SEEING THE
BIGGER
PICTURE

Dedicated to TCS with love

and a big thank you from the apprentice
to the sorcerer, Ben Schott

First published in Great Britain in 2012 by
Michael O'Mara Books Limited
9 Lion Yard
Tremadoc Road
London SW4 7NQ

A CIP catalogue record for this book is available from the British Library.

Papers used by Michael O'Mara Books Limited are natural,
recyclable products made from wood grown in sustainable
forests. The manufacturing processes conform to the
environmental regulations of the country of origin.

ISBN: 978-1-84317-786-9

1 2 3 4 5 6 7 8 9 10

www.mombooks.com

Cover design by Ana Bježančević

Designed and typeset by Ana Bježančević. With illustrations and
design work by Ron Callow, James Empringham, Anna Fidalgo, Siaron
Hughes, Sam Parij, Aubrey Smith, Greg Stevenson, William Renwick.

Printed by Tien Wah Press, Singapore

SEEING THE
BIGGER
PICTURE

GLOBAL INFOGRAPHICS

crime • happiness • religion • economics • defence spending
internet dating • mobile phones • and much more ...

CLAIRE COCK-STARKEY

Michael O'Mara Books Limited

CONTENTS

INTRODUCTION

Seeing The Bigger Picture covers a huge range of subjects including the environment, politics, overseas aid, crime and the economy – providing a truly global perspective on the issues that matter today. The data ranges from the serious to the quirky (and everything in between), each providing a different angle with which to compare and contrast countries around the world.

The data in the book can take you in many different directions – some facts might reveal the swings and roundabouts of a country's policies (for example, although China emits the most carbon dioxide in the world, it is also the country that invests the most in clean energy). Other facts confound expectations (alcohol causes more deaths worldwide per year than deaths from Aids or tuberculosis) and some facts ask more questions than they answer (Pakistan is host to the most refugees in the world with 1,900,600). Each set of data has been chosen to hold a mirror up to today's society.

A fact or figure alone can be enlightening, but put that fact in the correct context and it can bring a whole new level of understanding. You may take one piece of data and see that India had the greatest number of road fatalities in 2009 with 105,725 – but this figure is really put into perspective when compared with the 358 fatalities recorded in Sweden – population differences aside this is still a staggering difference in road safety.

In short, this book offers insights into the world we live in through a snapshot of comparative data and statistics presented as colourful infographics – allowing the reader to objectively look past their preconceptions, and see the bigger picture.

We hope you have as much fun reading it as we did putting it together.

LITERACY

% POPULATION OVER 15 THAT
CAN READ AND WRITE

▶ Men have a significantly higher
literacy rate than women – mainly
due to women's lack of access
to education. Nearly a billion
people worldwide started the
21st century unable to read a
book or sign their name.

Country	%
ETHIOPIA	30%
PAKISTAN	56%
BANGLADESH	56%
INDIA	63%
IRAQ	78%
KENYA	87%
SOUTH AFRICA	89%
MEXICO	93%
CHINA	94%
GREECE	97%
SPAIN	98%
SOUTH KOREA	98%
ARGENTINA	98%

▶ Roughly 72 million children of primary school age were not enrolled in school in 2005. One of the United Nations Development goals is that by 2015 all children around the world are able to complete their primary schooling.

▶ Sub-Saharan Africa has seen the greatest improvement in primary school enrolment – according to UN figures in 1998/9 just 58% of primary age children were in school but by 2008/9 this had improved to 76%.

USA	UK	SWEDEN	JAPAN	ITALY	GERMANY	FRANCE	AUSTRALIA	RUSSIA	POLAND
99%	99%	99%	99%	99%	99%	99%	99%	100%	100%

COMPUTERS

% OF POPULATION WHO USE COMPUTERS, 2007

▶ It is estimated that there were 1.4 billion computers in use worldwide in 2010. South Korea has the highest ownership of computers with 93% of people owning one, compared with just 2% in Bangladesh.

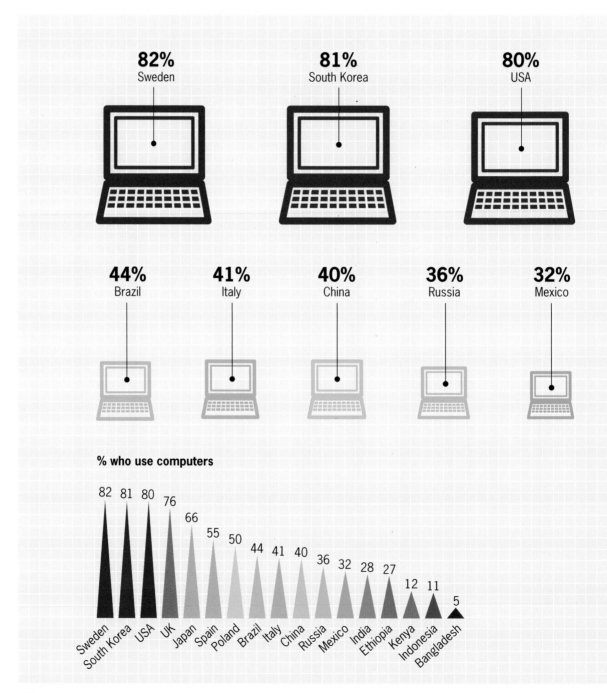

82%
Sweden

81%
South Korea

80%
USA

44%
Brazil

41%
Italy

40%
China

36%
Russia

32%
Mexico

% who use computers

82 Sweden
81 South Korea
80 USA
76 UK
66 Japan
55 Spain
50 Poland
44 Brazil
41 Italy
40 China
36 Russia
32 Mexico
28 India
27 Ethiopia
12 Kenya
11 Indonesia
5 Bangladesh

▶ Across Africa very few people own a computer but lots of people have access to computers – for example in the Ivory Coast just 6% of the population own a computer but 41% report using one at least occasionally.

▶ According to market research firm iSuppli, the top three PC manufacturers in 2011 were: Hewlett-Packard with 16.3 million global PC shipments; Lenovo with 12.5 million and Dell with 11.3 million.

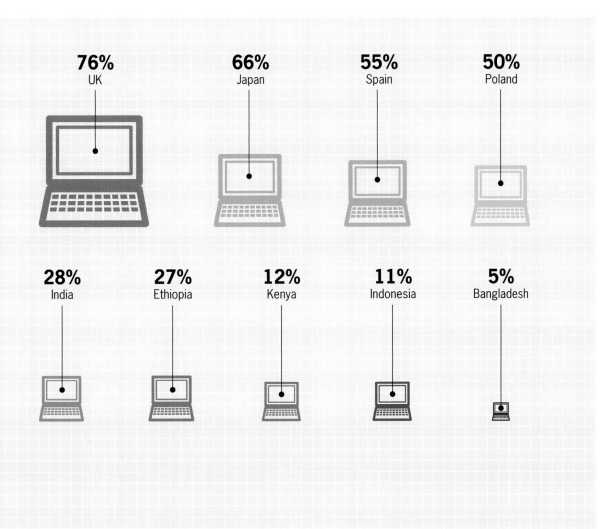

76%
UK

66%
Japan

55%
Spain

50%
Poland

28%
India

27%
Ethiopia

12%
Kenya

11%
Indonesia

5%
Bangladesh

N.B. Figures relate to those who say they use a computer at work, home or anywhere else at least occasionally.

GAMBLING

GAMBLING LOSSES PER
ADULT, 2011

▶ A 2011 study found that 70% of
Australians felt gambling should
be more controlled, the majority
favouring a method to allow
gamblers to set a spending limit
on slot machines before they
begin playing.

A♥
GAMBLING
ANNUAL
LOSSES PER
ADULT

$1,288
AUSTRALIA

$588
IRELAND

$568
CANADA

$503
HONG KONG

$448
NORWAY

The world's biggest lottery winner was American Andrew Whittaker who won £195 million in 2002. Europe's biggest lottery win came in 2011 when a couple from Scotland scooped £161 million on the Euro Millions lottery.

The Venetian casino in Macau, China, is the largest casino and the sixth biggest building in the world. It opened in 2007 and has 3,400 slot machines and 800 gambling tables. It is owned by the Las Vegas Sands Corporation.

$1,174
SINGAPORE

$553
FINLAND

$517
ITALY

$420
GREECE

$418
SPAIN

DRUNKENNESS

% 13–15-YEAR-OLDS
REPEATEDLY DRUNK, 2009

▶ Alcohol consumption in Europe is the highest in the world. Drinking alcohol can begin very early, for example in the Ukraine 24% of 11-year-old boys and 20% of 11-year-old girls drink alcohol at least once a week.

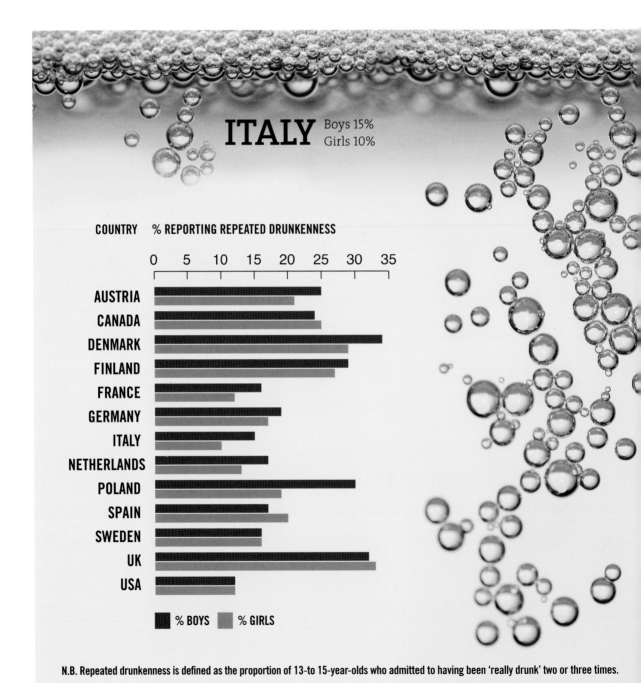

ITALY Boys 15% Girls 10%

COUNTRY   % REPORTING REPEATED DRUNKENNESS

AUSTRIA
CANADA
DENMARK
FINLAND
FRANCE
GERMANY
ITALY
NETHERLANDS
POLAND
SPAIN
SWEDEN
UK
USA

■ % BOYS   ■ % GIRLS

N.B. Repeated drunkenness is defined as the proportion of 13-to 15-year-olds who admitted to having been 'really drunk' two or three times.

▶ Teens drinking alcohol is associated with lots of other risky behaviours, such as drug taking, fighting and having unprotected sex. In the USA 2,000 people die every year as a result of car crashes caused by underage drinkers.

▶ Drinking does not always lead to drunkenness. For 15-and 16-year-olds in Southern Europe one in ten drinking occasions result in drunkenness, compared to nearly five in ten in the USA. Globally, boys drink more commonly than girls.

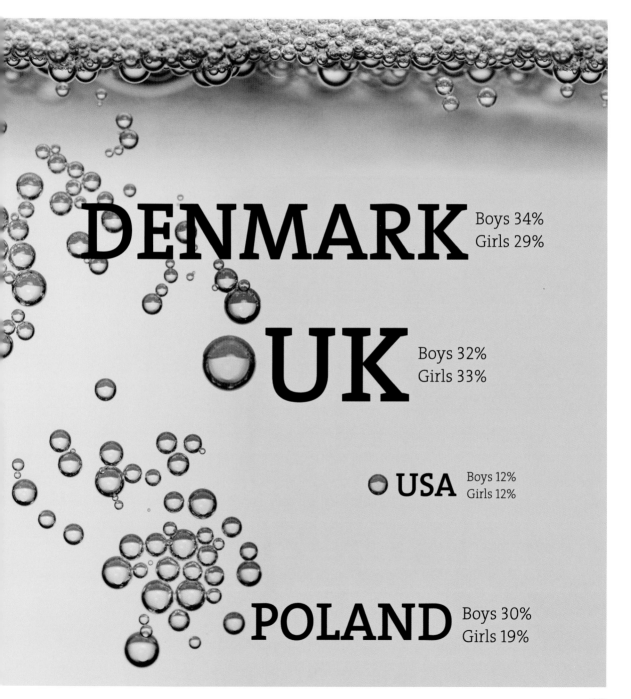

DENMARK Boys 34%
Girls 29%

UK Boys 32%
Girls 33%

USA Boys 12%
Girls 12%

POLAND Boys 30%
Girls 19%

WORK

ANNUAL HOURS WORKED PER PERSON, 2010

▶ Living in the hardest working country in the world, many South Koreans work a six day week and are given only three days of holiday a year. Mexicans have the longest average working day, clocking up 9.54 hours of work.

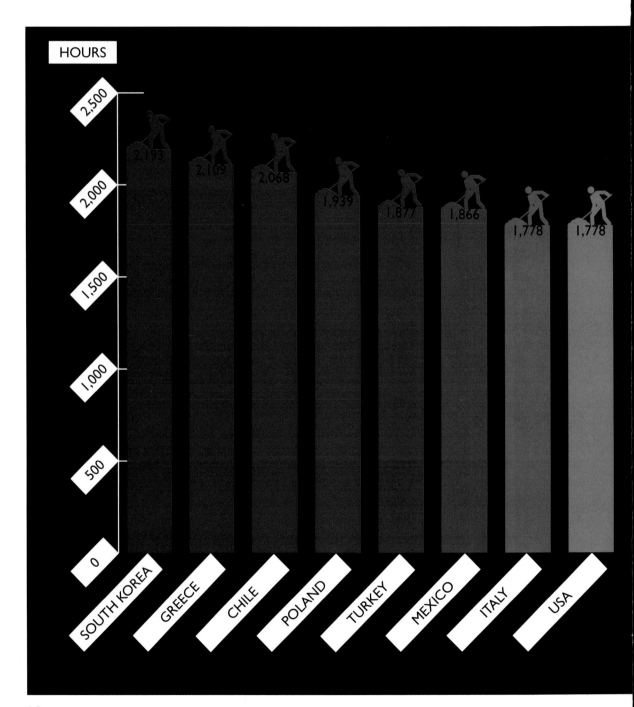

HOURS

2,500
2,000
1,500
1,000
500
0

SOUTH KOREA	GREECE	CHILE	POLAND	TURKEY	MEXICO	ITALY	USA
2,193	2,109	2,068	1,939	1,877	1,866	1,778	1,778

- In the 1970s Europeans worked longer hours than Americans but this trend has changed. Since the 1960s, European working hours have reduced by 23% compared to American hours which have only reduced by 3%.

- The USA has the smallest annual leave entitlement in the industrialized world. The average American is entitled to just 13 days holiday, compared to 42 days in Italy, 37 in France, 35 in Germany and 34 in Brazil.

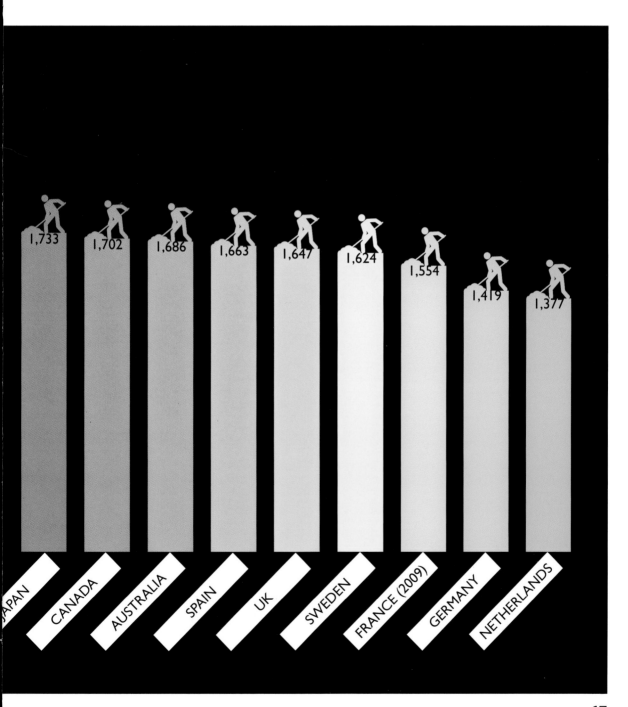

CARS

PASSENGER CARS
PER 1,000 PEOPLE, 2008

▶ There were an estimated 622 million passenger cars worldwide in 2008, compared to 500 million in the year 2000. The world's most congested city is São Paulo, Brazil, where a record 165-mile tailback was recorded in 2008.

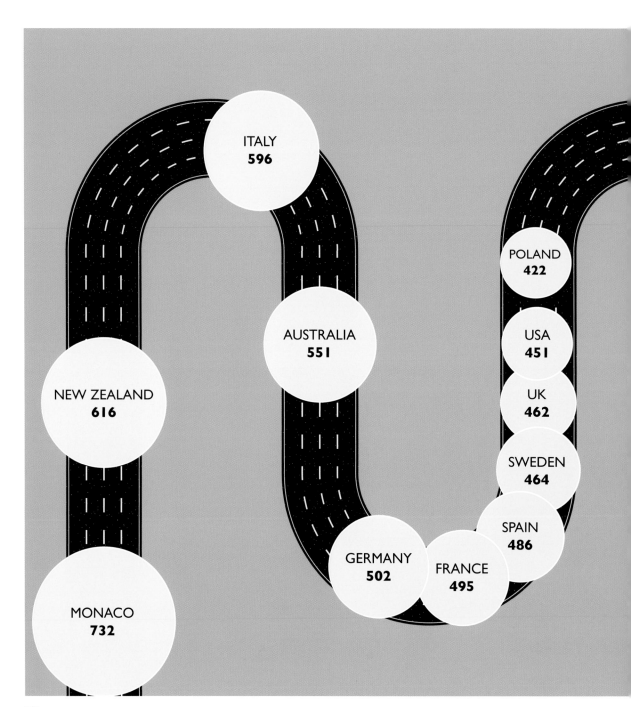

ITALY
596

POLAND
422

AUSTRALIA
551

USA
451

NEW ZEALAND
616

UK
462

SWEDEN
464

SPAIN
486

GERMANY
502

FRANCE
495

MONACO
732

▶ In 2007 Japan produced the most vehicles globally with 11 million units, with the USA right behind on 10.5 million. China produced 8.4 million, followed by Germany with 6 million and South Korea with 4 million.

▶ The top ten bestselling cars in the world during 2009 were: Toyota Corolla; Ford Focus; Ford Fiesta; Volkswagen Golf; Honda Civic; Toyota Camry; Honda Accord; Peugeot 207; Volkswagen Polo; and the Toyota Yaris.

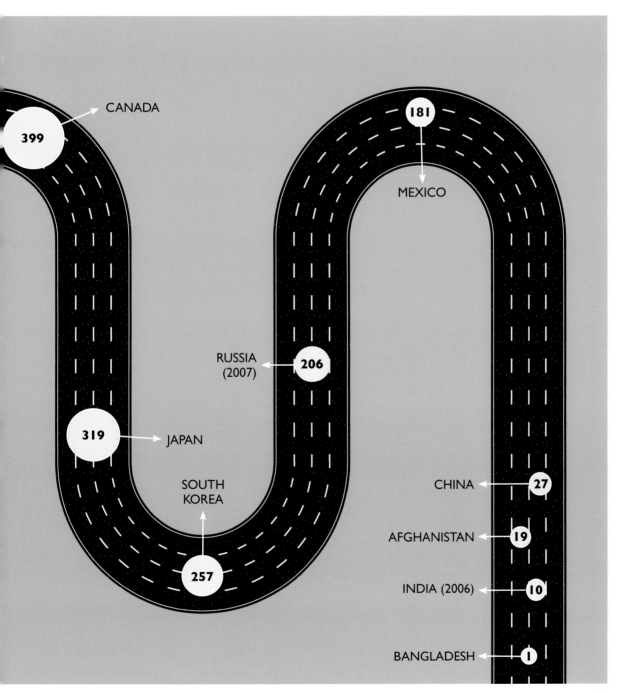

HERITAGE SITES

UNESCO WORLD
HERITAGE SITES, 2012

▶ The World Heritage List was
agreed in 1972. In 1978 the first
twelve sites were inscribed – these
included: the Galapagos Islands;
Aachen Cathedral, Germany;
Simien National Park, Ethiopia; and
Yellowstone National Park, USA.

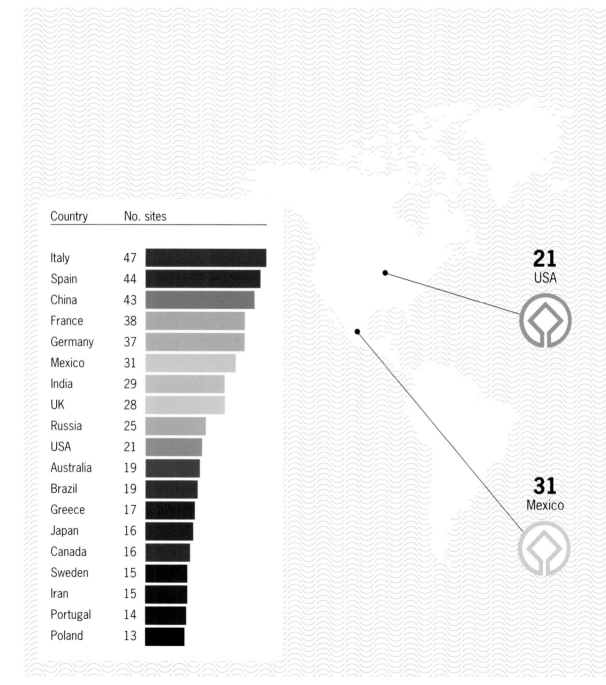

Country	No. sites
Italy	47
Spain	44
China	43
France	38
Germany	37
Mexico	31
India	29
UK	28
Russia	25
USA	21
Australia	19
Brazil	19
Greece	17
Japan	16
Canada	16
Sweden	15
Iran	15
Portugal	14
Poland	13

21
USA

31
Mexico

▶ There are currently 936 cultural and natural sites listed as UNESCO World Heritage Sites – places that the committee believes have 'outstanding universal value'. Each year new sites are added – in 2011 25 new sites were inscribed.

▶ Since 1978 two sites have been delisted – Oman's Arabian Oryx Sanctuary, after Oman's protection for 90% of the sanctuary was reneged when oil was found, and Germany's Dresden Elbe Valley after a bridge was built.

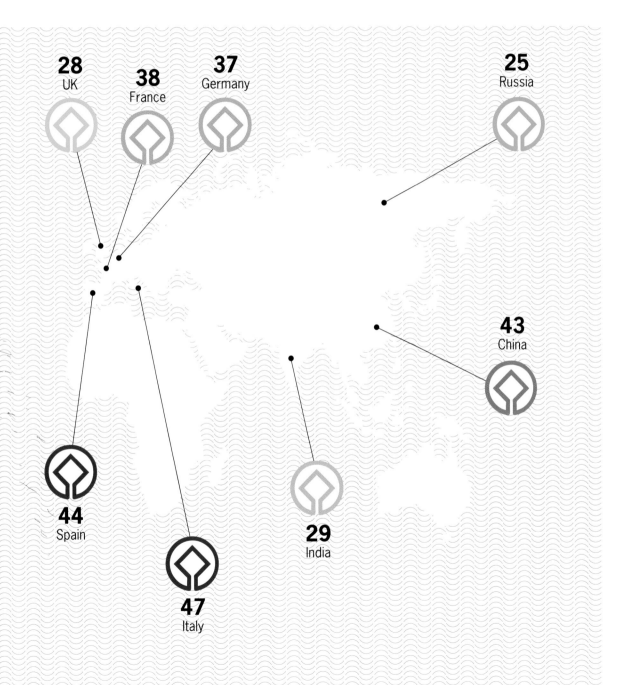

28
UK

38
France

37
Germany

25
Russia

43
China

44
Spain

47
Italy

29
India

30%

of the world's ice-free land is devoted to the direct or indirect production of livestock, a figure that is increasing to feed the world's growing appetite for meat.

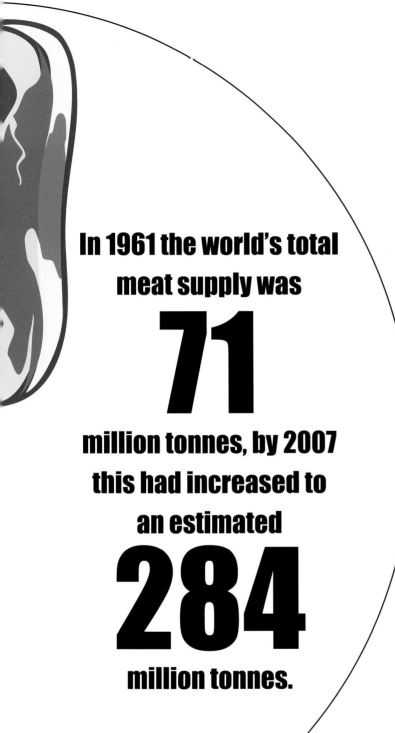

In 1961 the world's total
meat supply was

71

million tonnes, by 2007
this had increased to
an estimated

284

million tonnes.

LEADERS

LONGEST-SERVING POLITICAL LEADERS, 2012

▶ King Bhumibol Adulyadej of Thailand is the world's longest-serving monarch, with a 65 year reign. The longest of all time was King Sobhuza II of Swaziland, who was throned in 1899 and ruled until his death in 1982.

Country	Ruled for (years)
Bahrain	42
Zimbabwe	32
Iran	31
Cameroon	30
Uganda	27
Sudan	23
Uzbekistan	23
Kazakhstan	22
Ethiopia	21

42 years

Prime Minister Khalifa bin Salman Al Khalifa (Bahrain)

27 years

President Yoweri Museveni (Uganda)

23 years

President Omar al-Bashir (Sudan)

▶ Robert Mugabe topped *Parade* magazine's list of the world's worst dictators, 2009. The rest of the top ten consisted of the following: Omar Al-Bashir of Sudan, Kim Jong-Il of North Korea, Than Shwe of Myanmar, King Abdullah of Saudi Arabia, Hu Jintao of China, Ali Khamenei of Iran, Isayas Afewerki of Eritrea, Gurbanguly Berdymukhammedov of Turkmenistan and Muammar Gaddafi of Libya.

32 years

President Robert
Mugabe
(Zimbabwe)

31 years

Supreme Leader
Ali Khamenei
(Iran)

30 years

President Paul Biya
(Cameroon)

23 years

President Islam
Karimov
(Uzbekistan)

22 years

President Nursultan
Nazarbayev
(Kazakhstan)

21 years

Prime Minister
Meles Zenawi
(Ethiopia)

HOMICIDE

NUMBER OF HOMICIDES PER
100,000 PEOPLE, 2010

▶ Worldwide, young men are the
most likely victims of intentional
homicide, with a rate of 11.9 per
100,000 people, compared to a rate
of 2.6 per 100,000 for women.

#4
COUNTRY:
JAMAICA
HOMICIDE RATE:
52.1
NO. OF
HOMICIDES:
1,428

#1
COUNTRY:
HONDURAS
HOMICIDE RATE:
82.1
NO. OF
HOMICIDES:
6,239

#9
COUNTRY:
ETHIOPIA
HOMICIDE RATE:
25.5
NO. OF
HOMICIDES:
20,239

#5
COUNTRY:
VENEZUELA
HOMICIDE RATE:
49
NO. OF
HOMICIDES:
13,985

#8
COUNTRY:
COLOMBIA
HOMICIDE RATE:
33.4
NO. OF
HOMICIDES:
15,459

▶ By contrast, women are most at risk of homicide resulting from domestic violence. In 2008 women made up almost 80% of victims killed by a current or former partner.

▶ Proliferation of guns in Central America and the Caribbean has meant roughly 75% of homicides are carried out with a firearm, compared with 21% in Europe.

#2
COUNTRY:
EL SALVADOR
HOMICIDE RATE:
66
NO. OF HOMICIDES:
4,085

#3
COUNTRY:
COTE D'IVOIRE
HOMICIDE RATE:
56.9
NO. OF HOMICIDES:
10,801

#10
COUNTRY:
BRAZIL
HOMICIDE RATE:
22.7
NO. OF HOMICIDES:
43,909

#6
COUNTRY:
UGANDA
HOMICIDE RATE:
36.3
NO. OF HOMICIDES:
11,303

#7
COUNTRY:
SOUTH AFRICA
HOMICIDE RATE:
33.8
NO. OF HOMICIDES:
16,834

BILLIONAIRES

NUMBER OF BILLIONAIRES PER
COUNTRY, 2011

▶ The richest man in the world is Mexican telecoms tycoon Carlos Slim Helu, with an estimated fortune of $74 billion. He first topped the list in 2010, the first non-American to do so in 16 years.

CANADA
24

USA
413

BRAZIL
30

- Moscow has the most billionaires in residence with 79, New York has 59 and London is third with 41. There are a reported 1,210 billionaires in the world, with a net worth of $4.5 trillion.

- The world's youngest billionaire is Dustin Moskovitz, co-founder of Facebook, with an estimated $2.7 billion. Seven people on the 2011 Rich List made their fortunes through Facebook.

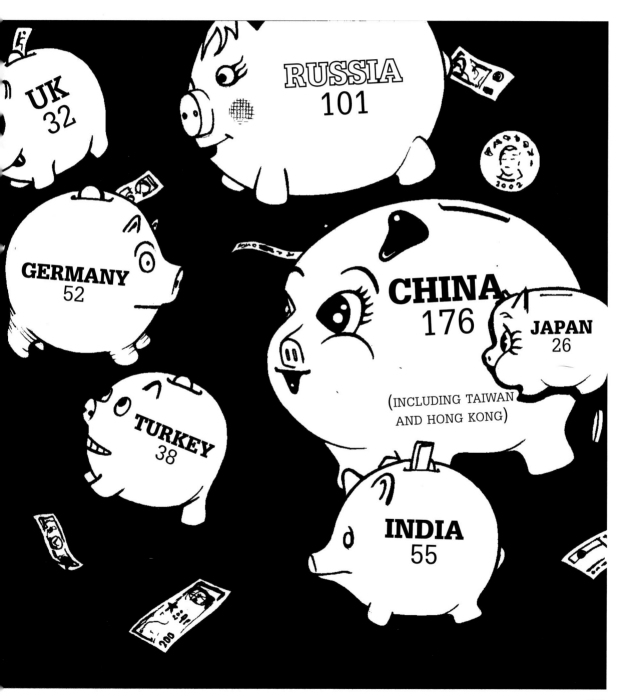

IN 2012 THE WORLD'S GOVERNMENTS COLLECTIVELY HELD APPROXIMATELY

$45

TRILLION OF DEBT.

THIS COMPARES TO THE WORLD'S COLLECTIVE GROSS DOMESTIC PRODUCT (GDP) OF

$65

TRILLION.

INCOME

ANNUAL HOUSEHOLD
DISPOSABLE INCOME, 2011

▶ The richest 25% of the world's population receive 75% of the world's income. More than 1 billion people worldwide live on less than $1 a day according to charity World Vision.

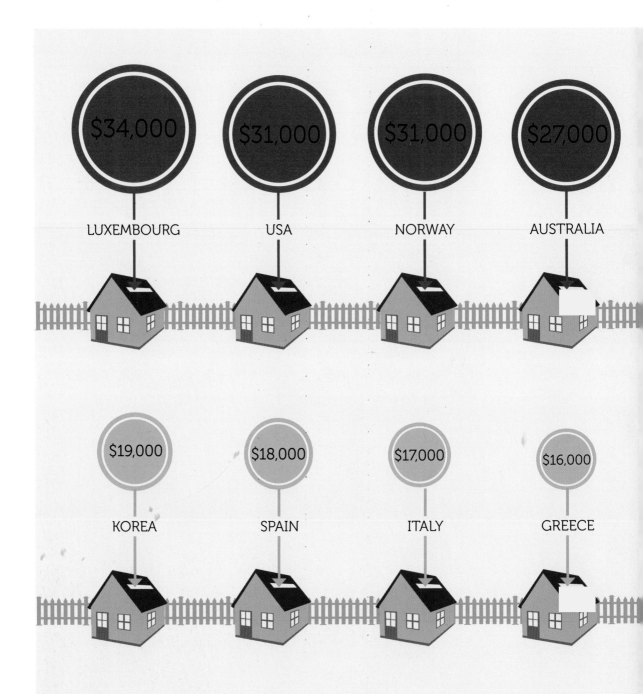

| LUXEMBOURG | USA | NORWAY | AUSTRALIA |
| $34,000 | $31,000 | $31,000 | $27,000 |

| KOREA | SPAIN | ITALY | GREECE |
| $19,000 | $18,000 | $17,000 | $16,000 |

In the last 25 years many rich countries such as those in Western Europe, USA and Australia have grown richer, whereas those living in Eastern Europe and sub-Saharan Africa have grown poorer.

According to the United Nations, the world's poorest countries (those with the lowest levels of human development) are mostly in Africa, with Zimbabwe at the bottom of the list.

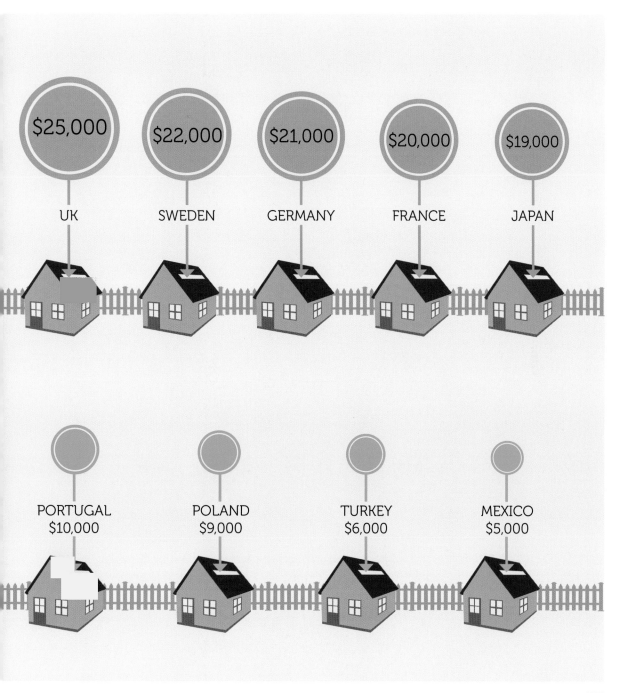

$25,000

$22,000

$21,000

$20,000

$19,000

UK

SWEDEN

GERMANY

FRANCE

JAPAN

PORTUGAL
$10,000

POLAND
$9,000

TURKEY
$6,000

MEXICO
$5,000

CLEAN ENERGY

TOP 10 INVESTORS IN CLEAN ENERGY, 2010

▶ There was a record $243 billion investment in clean energy sources in 2010. 90% of all clean energy investments were made by the world's top economies – the G20. Of these nations, the USA was the biggest investor.

TOP 10 INVESTORS

1.	CHINA	$54.4BN
2.	GERMANY	$41.2BN
3.	USA	$34BN
4.	ITALY	$13.9BN
5.	BRAZIL	$7.6BN
6.	CANADA	$5.6BN
7.	SPAIN	$4.9BN
8.	FRANCE	$4BN
9.	INDIA	$4BN
10.	JAPAN	$3.5BN

CHINA: **$54.4BN**

ITALY: **$13.9BN**

SPAIN: **$4.9BN**

JAPAN: **$3.5BN**

▶ Europe was the leading recipient of clean energy investment in 2010, with the majority going to small scale solar installations. Most investments in 2010 went into solar energy, with a 53% increase in investment since 2009.

▶ Worldwide clean energy generating power capacity reached 338 gW in 2010. A report issued in 2012 forecast that private investments in G20 clean power projects could total $2.3 trillion by the end of the decade.

GERMANY: **$41.2BN**

USA: **$34BN**

FRANCE: **$4BN**

CANADA: **$5.6BN**

INDIA: **$4BN**

BRAZIL: **$7.6BN**

LEISURE

% TIME SPENT ON LEISURE PER DAY, 2006

▶ 'Personal care' (eating, sleeping, personal hygiene etc) took up the majority of people's leisure time, from a low of 42.7% of leisure time in Mexico to a high of 49.2% in France.

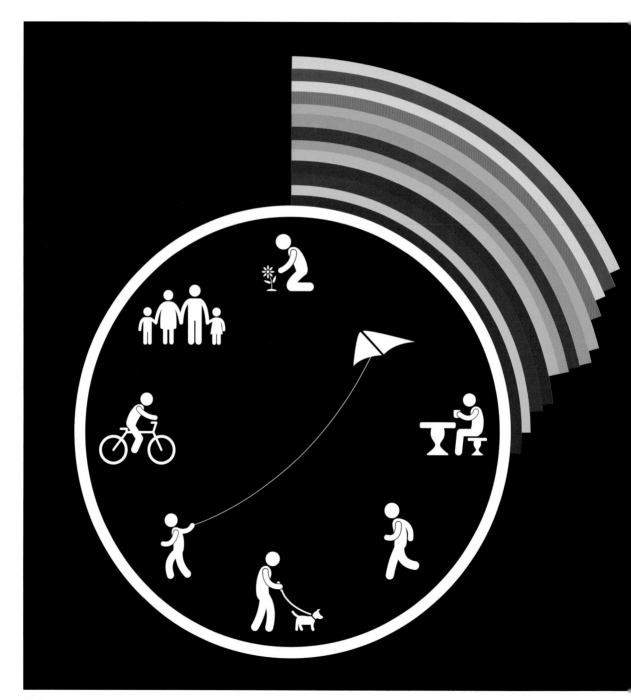

- On average, people sleep for 8 hours and 22 minutes a day and spend 1 hour 37 minutes on eating. The French and Americans get the most sleep, with the Japanese and South Koreans getting the least.

- France also spends most time eating (but is one of the least obese) followed by New Zealand and Japan. The countries that spend the least time eating are Mexico, Canada and the USA.

NORWAY **26.5%**

GERMANY **25%**

SWEDEN **23.7%**

UK **23.4%**

USA **21.7%**

SPAIN **21.7%**

SOUTH KOREA **21.6%**

POLAND **21.4%**

ITALY **21.1%**

AUSTRALIA **19.6%**

TURKEY **18.7%**

FRANCE **18.4%**

JAPAN **18%**

LEISURE ACTIVITIES DEFINED AS:
hobbies, games, TV, computer use, sport and socializing.

LIFE EXPECTANCY

LIFE EXPECTANCY AT BIRTH,
2011 ESTIMATE

▶ Lifespan is double what it was 200 years ago and increases at a rate of roughly two years per decade. The lifespan of an average Angolan (38 years) is the same as the lifespan of an unskilled worker living in the 19th century.

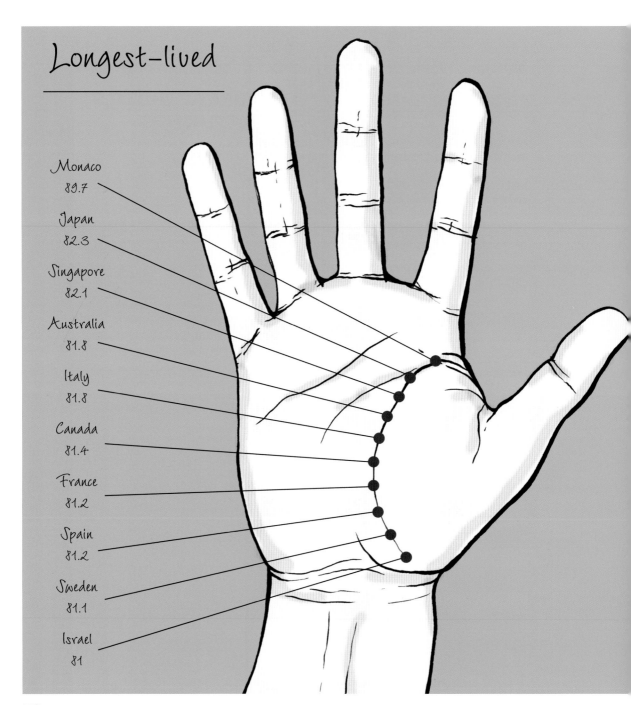

Longest-lived

Monaco
89.7

Japan
82.3

Singapore
82.1

Australia
81.8

Italy
81.8

Canada
81.4

France
81.2

Spain
81.2

Sweden
81.1

Israel
81

▶ The United Nations forecast that the 7 billionth person on our planet would be born on 31st October 2011. It has taken just twelve years for the global population to grow from 6 billion to a new high of 7 billion.

▶ Scientists currently suggest that 150 might be a realistic lifespan for many humans alive today. Researchers at the University of California were able to extend the lifespan of worms by 900% by partially disabling a single gene.

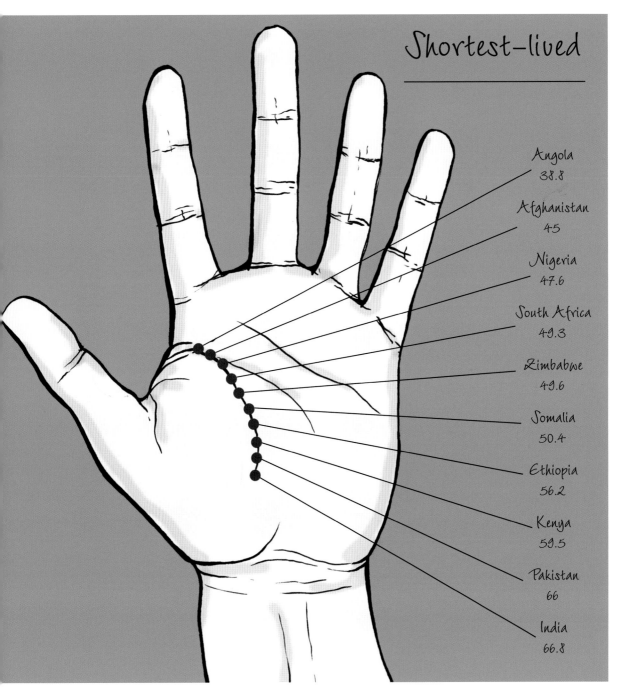

Shortest-lived

Angola
38.8

Afghanistan
45

Nigeria
47.6

South Africa
49.3

Zimbabwe
49.6

Somalia
50.4

Ethiopia
56.2

Kenya
59.5

Pakistan
66

India
66.8

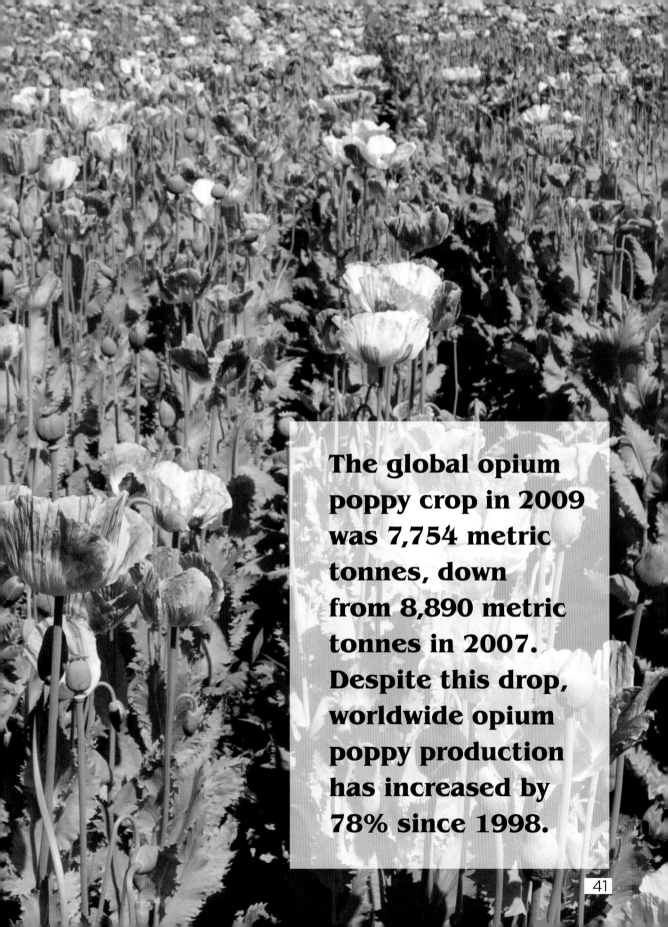

The global opium poppy crop in 2009 was 7,754 metric tonnes, down from 8,890 metric tonnes in 2007. Despite this drop, worldwide opium poppy production has increased by 78% since 1998.

ELECTRICITY

% POPULATION WITH ACCESS TO ELECTRICITY, 2009

▶ 1.3 billion people, roughly 20% of the world's population, are without electricity. There is a divide between the world's urban and rural population – worldwide the electrification rate is 94% for urban areas but only 68% for rural areas.

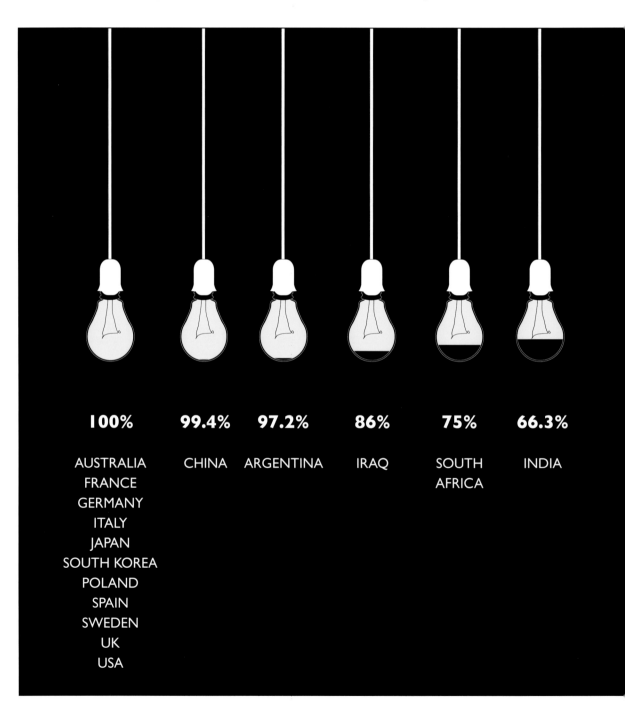

100%	99.4%	97.2%	86%	75%	66.3%
AUSTRALIA	CHINA	ARGENTINA	IRAQ	SOUTH AFRICA	INDIA
FRANCE					
GERMANY					
ITALY					
JAPAN					
SOUTH KOREA					
POLAND					
SPAIN					
SWEDEN					
UK					
USA					

▶ In Africa 571 million people are without electricity but there is a sharp north-south divide – in North Africa 99% of people have access to electricity but in sub-Saharan Africa only 31% of the population has access to electricity.

▶ Energy has become vital to modern human life and as such the International Energy Agency states that an individual's access to electricity is one of the clearest indicators of a country's energy poverty status.

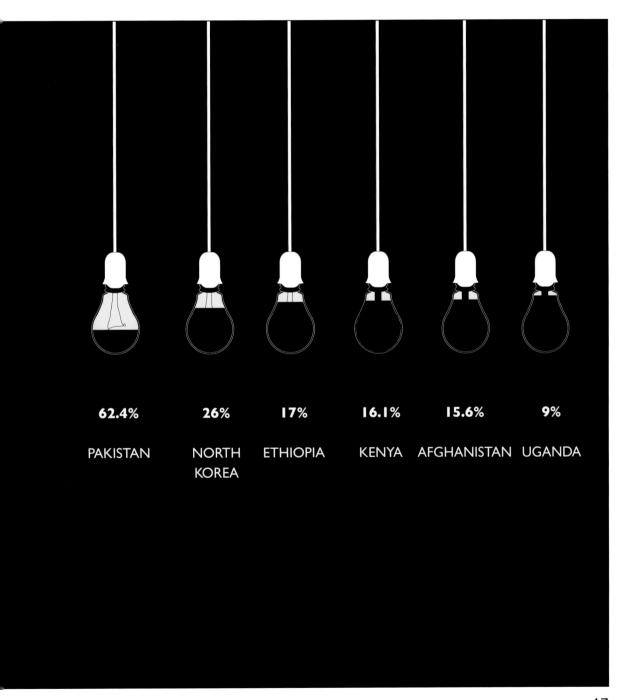

| 62.4% | 26% | 17% | 16.1% | 15.6% | 9% |
| PAKISTAN | NORTH KOREA | ETHIOPIA | KENYA | AFGHANISTAN | UGANDA |

ARABLE LAND

% LAND USED FOR GROWING CROPS, 2005

▶ 11% of the world's land is given over to arable crops. China is the world's biggest producer of wheat, followed by India and USA. Worldwide, twice the amount of land is used as animal pasture as is for the production of crops.

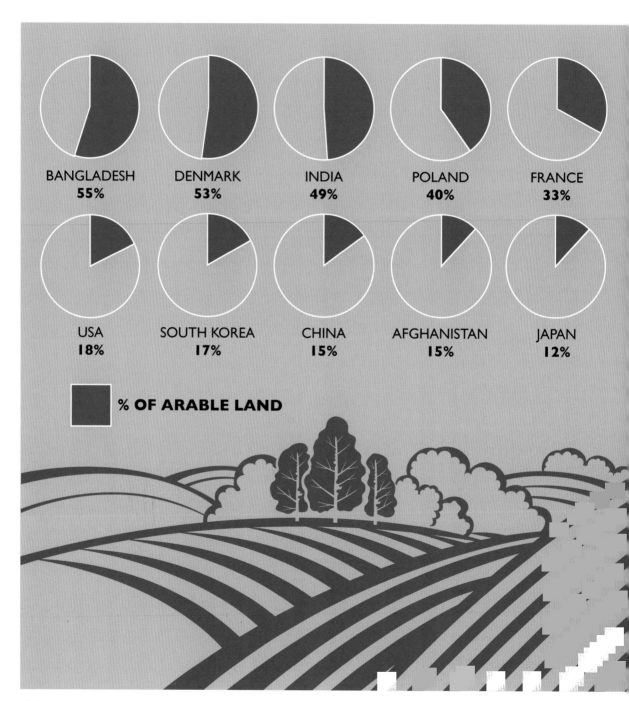

BANGLADESH
55%

DENMARK
53%

INDIA
49%

POLAND
40%

FRANCE
33%

USA
18%

SOUTH KOREA
17%

CHINA
15%

AFGHANISTAN
15%

JAPAN
12%

% OF ARABLE LAND

▶ Rich countries are buying arable land in poor countries as they can't grow enough food to support themselves. In 2009 South Korea bought 700,000ha in Sudan and Saudi Arabia purchased 500,000ha in Tanzania.

▶ Livestock production produces less protein per hectare than grain production, however animals can often be successfully raised on marginal land that would not otherwise be used for food production.

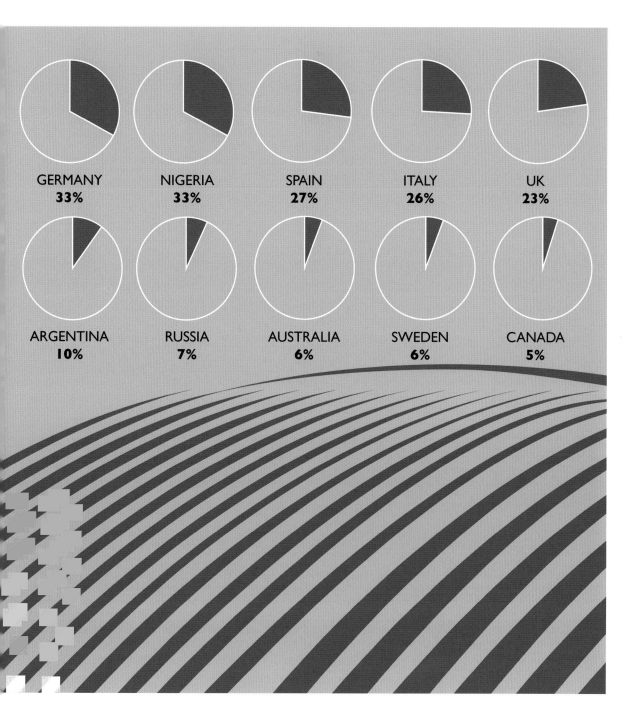

| GERMANY 33% | NIGERIA 33% | SPAIN 27% | ITALY 26% | UK 23% |

| ARGENTINA 10% | RUSSIA 7% | AUSTRALIA 6% | SWEDEN 6% | CANADA 5% |

SEX LIFE

% KNOWING HOW TO HAVE
A FULFILLING SEX LIFE, 2008

▶ On average, women tend to lose their virginity at 18.9 years, compared to 19.5 for men. China has the oldest mean age at which they first received formal sex education at 15.4, Mexico has the youngest at 12.1.

MOST CONFIDENT

Brazil (79.6%)   **Mexico** (78.4%)   **Nigeria** (78.2%)

▶ The 2008 Durex Sex Survey questioned people from 26 countries and discovered that those from most Asian countries were less confident about how to avoid unwanted pregnancy compared to those from western nations.

▶ Women are 28% more likely than men to use contraception when they first have sex. Only 42% of Japanese had confidence in knowing where to look for guidance on sex, compared to 80% of people in Brazil.

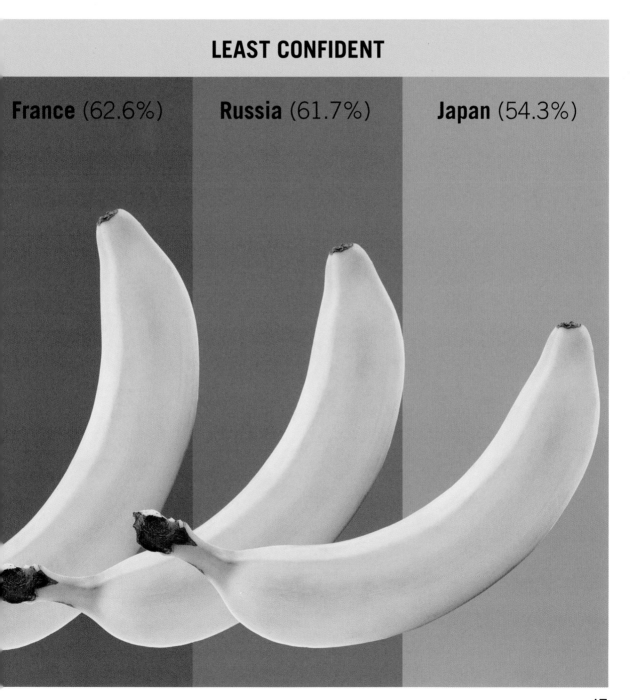

LEAST CONFIDENT

France (62.6%) **Russia** (61.7%) **Japan** (54.3%)

INFANT MORTALITY

DEATHS PER 1000, 2011
ESTIMATE

▶ Infant mortality is the number of deaths of children under one year old for every 1,000 live births. The world average is 43 for 2010–15, compared to 152 in 1950–55.

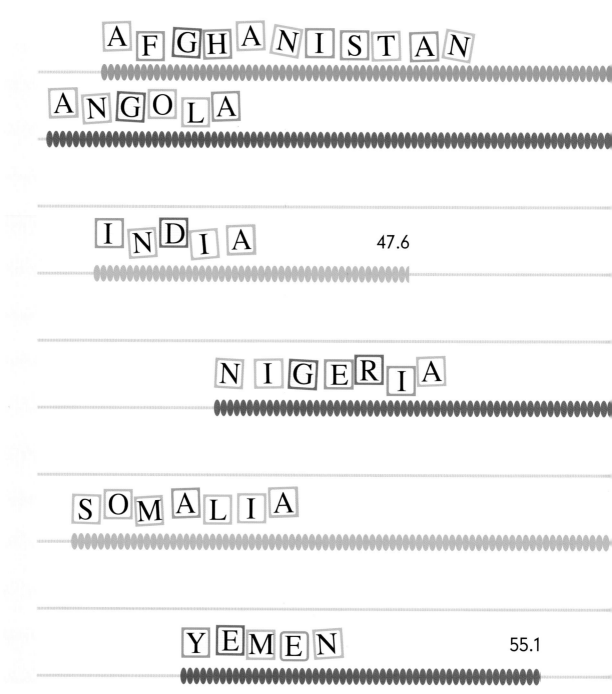

AFGHANISTAN

ANGOLA

INDIA   47.6

NIGERIA

SOMALIA

YEMEN   55.1

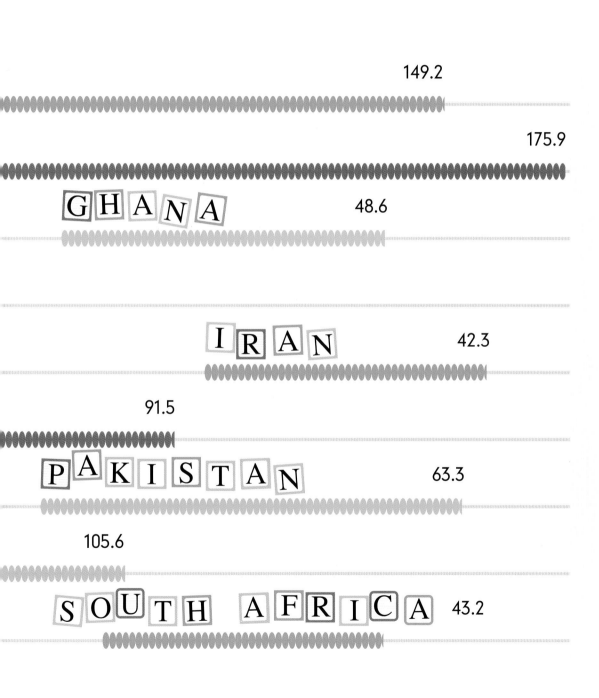

149.2

175.9

GHANA 48.6

IRAN 42.3

91.5

PAKISTAN 63.3

105.6

SOUTH AFRICA 43.2

OVERSEAS AID

RECIPIENTS OF AID IN
MILLIONS (US $, 2009)

▶ Since 1970 the top five donors
of Overseas Development Aid
have been USA, Germany, UK,
France and Japan. In 2009 5%
of all Overseas Development Aid
for developing countries went to
Afghanistan.

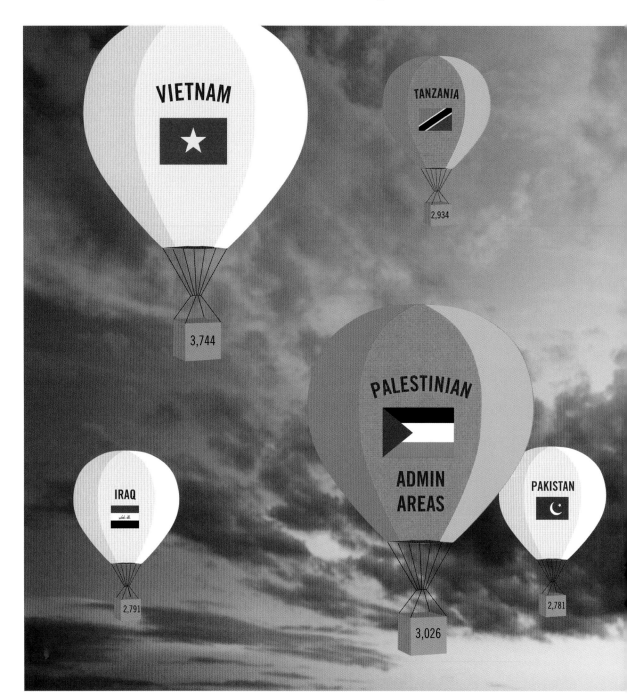

VIETNAM
3,744

TANZANIA
2,934

PALESTINIAN
ADMIN
AREAS
3,026

IRAQ
2,791

PAKISTAN
2,781

Africa received the greatest share of Overseas Development Aid, taking $47,609 million. This was followed by Asia with $38,333 million, America with $9,089 million, Europe with $5,788 million and Oceania with $1,647 million.

If you compare aid received with the population of each region it shows that by aid received per person in 2009, Oceania actually received the most with $184 going to each person. Africa was second with $47 per person.

According to NASA, nine of the ten warmest years

on record since 1880 have occurred since the year 2000.

NOBEL PRIZE

COUNTRIES WITH THE MOST
NOBEL PRIZE WINNERS, 2011

▶ Between 1901 and 2011 the Nobel prizes in Physics, Chemistry, Medicine, Literature and Peace have been awarded 549 times. Only 40 women have ever won Nobel prizes.

0-15	
Austria	14
Denmark	11
Australia	10
Norway	10
China	8

16-49	
Sweden	28
Russia	24
Poland	20
Italy	19
Netherlands	17
Switzerland	17
Canada	16
Japan	16

▶ Australian Lawrence Bragg, aged 25, was the youngest ever winner, he claimed the 1915 Physics prize jointly with his father, William. Each Nobel winner receives a medal, a personal diploma and a cash prize.

▶ In 2011 each Nobel prize was worth 10 million Swedish Kroner (c. £973,000) to the winner. 830 individuals and 23 organizations have been awarded a Nobel prize since its inception.

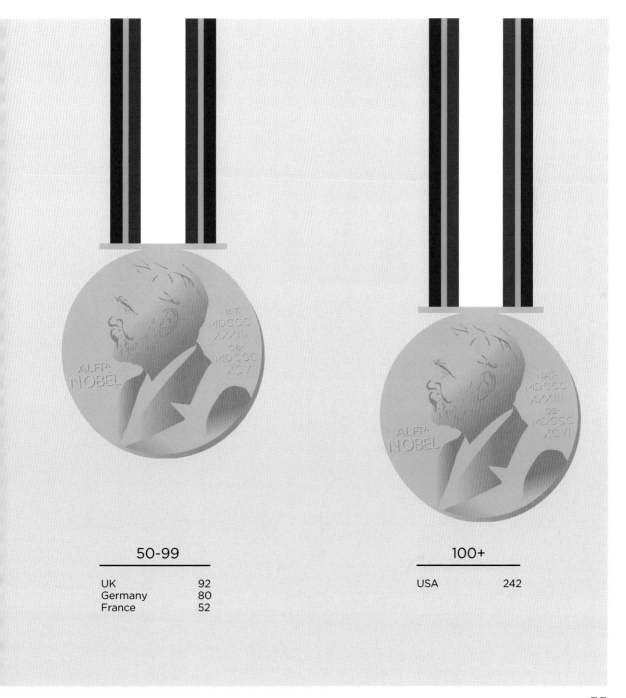

50-99	
UK	92
Germany	80
France	52

100+	
USA	242

ECONOMY

% SATISFACTION WITH OUTLOOK OF COUNTRY, 2011

▶ When asked if they felt China would replace USA as the world's leading superpower, 15 of the 22 nations questioned believed that China would overtake the USA or already has overtaken the USA.

PAKISTAN
- 6% satisfied with country direction
- 12% good current economic situation

CHINA

- 85% satisfied with country direction
- 88% good current economic situation

EGYPT

- 65% satisfied with country direction
- 34% good current economic situation

UKRAINE
- 9% satisfied with country direction
- 6% good current economic situation

▶ Whilst China is seen as catching up on the USA, the majority in many countries (including: Japan 55%, China 50%, Turkey 68%) still see the USA as the world's leading economic superpower.

▶ Asked if their economy would improve, the majority in China (84%) and Brazil (79%) thought it would, whereas in Pakistan (60%), Japan (52%) and France (52%) felt it would worsen.

BRAZIL

KENYA
- 19% satisfied with country direction
- 26% good current economic situation

- 52% satisfied with country direction
- 54% good current economic situation

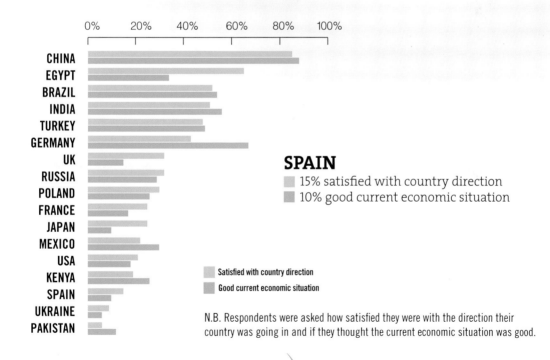

SPAIN
- 15% satisfied with country direction
- 10% good current economic situation

Satisfied with country direction

Good current economic situation

N.B. Respondents were asked how satisfied they were with the direction their country was going in and if they thought the current economic situation was good.

MAMMALS

MAMMAL SPECIES UNDER
THREAT, 2010

▶ The Red List is a database of
threatened species. In December
2011 it had 3,879 species on
its Critically Endangered list,
including the Mediterranean
Monk Seal of which there are
only 350-450 left in the wild.

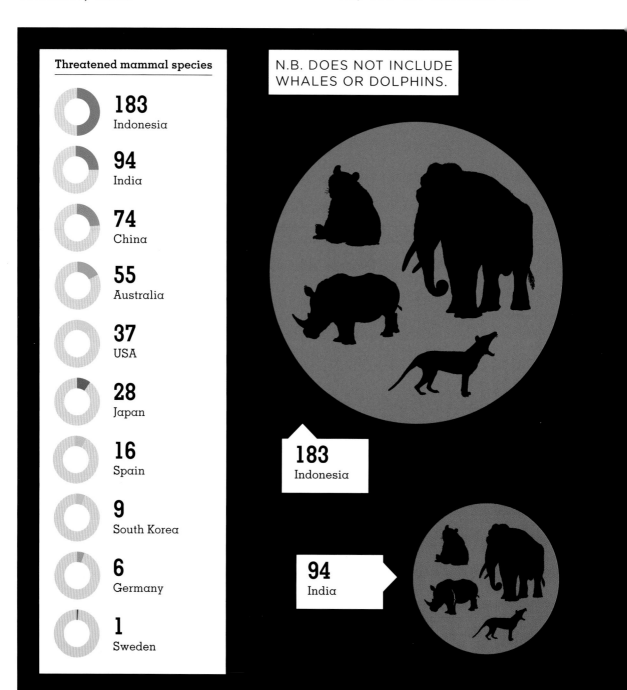

Threatened mammal species

183 Indonesia

94 India

74 China

55 Australia

37 USA

28 Japan

16 Spain

9 South Korea

6 Germany

1 Sweden

N.B. DOES NOT INCLUDE
WHALES OR DOLPHINS.

183 Indonesia

94 India

▶ In 2010 the top ten most endangered animals were: tigers, polar bears; Pacific walrus; Magellanic penguins; leatherback turtles; bluefin tuna; mountain gorillas; monarch butterflies; Javan rhinos and giant pandas.

▶ Conservationists have seen success in rescuing species from the brink, for example the Southern White Rhino, which had a dwindling population of just 100 at the end of the 19th century, but now has a wild population of about 20,000.

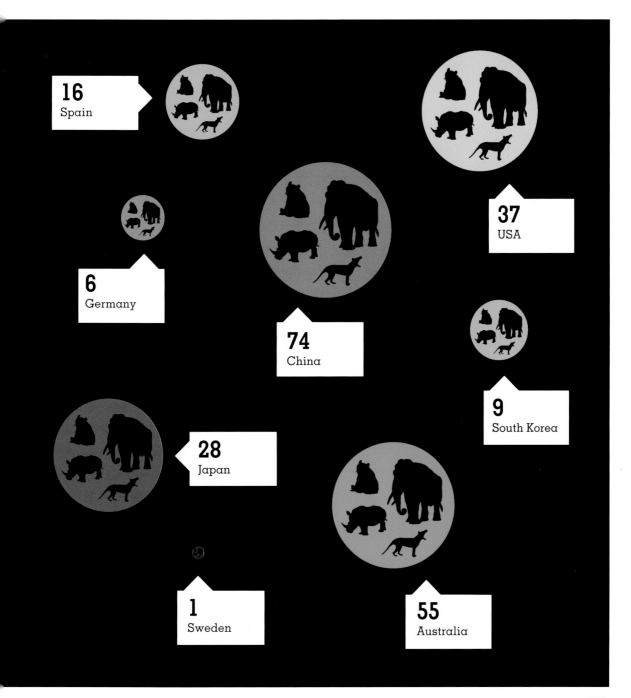

16
Spain

37
USA

6
Germany

74
China

9
South Korea

28
Japan

1
Sweden

55
Australia

CITY LIVING

% OF POPULATION LIVING IN URBAN AREAS, 2008

▶ In 1800 only 3% of the world's population lived in an urban area, but by 2008 over half of the world's population (some 3.3 billion people) did. It is estimated that by 2030 over 5 billion will.

- As a result of such fast growth, poverty is now generally more of a problem in urban rather than rural areas, with the United Nations estimating that 1 billion people worldwide now live in urban slums.

- Many environmentalists believe that a move by the population to cities is good for the environment as city dwellers tend to have a lower carbon footprint than their rural neighbours.

NUCLEAR

PRODUCERS OF NUCLEAR POWER, 2010

▶ In 2008, 13.4% of the world's total electricity came from nuclear power. This compares with other sources of energy: coal (40.8%), gas (21.3%), hydro (16.2%), oil (5.5%) and other (2.8%).

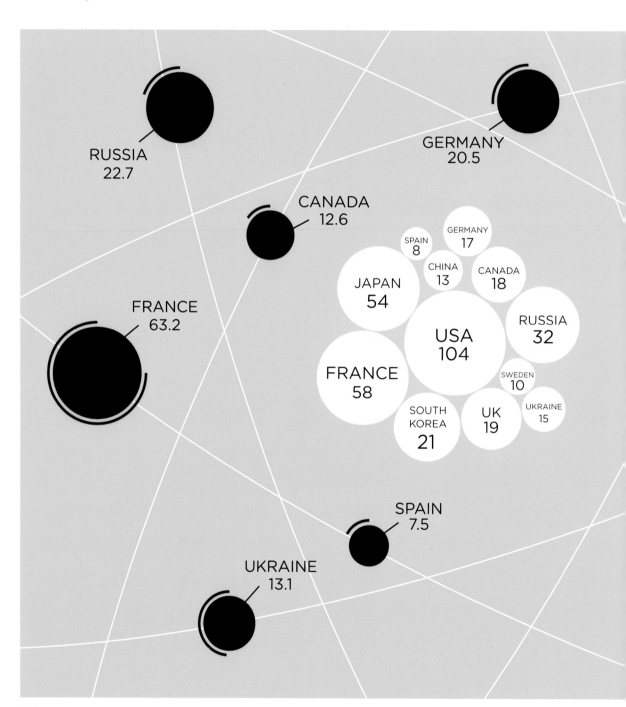

RUSSIA
22.7

GERMANY
20.5

CANADA
12.6

FRANCE
63.2

SPAIN
8

GERMANY
17

CHINA
13

CANADA
18

JAPAN
54

USA
104

RUSSIA
32

FRANCE
58

SWEDEN
10

SOUTH
KOREA
21

UK
19

UKRAINE
15

SPAIN
7.5

UKRAINE
13.1

▶ There are 440 nuclear power reactors in thirty different countries. Sixty new nuclear power plants worldwide are currently under construction, with the majority being built in China.

▶ There have been eleven serious nuclear reactor accidents since the inception of nuclear power, the most serious being that at Chernobyl in 1986 and the most recent at Fukushima, Japan, in 2011.

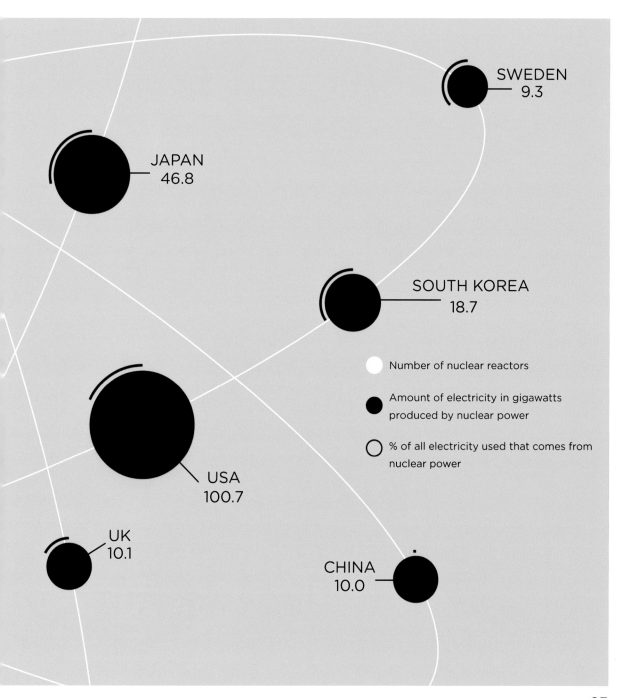

SWEDEN
9.3

JAPAN
46.8

SOUTH KOREA
18.7

○ Number of nuclear reactors

● Amount of electricity in gigawatts produced by nuclear power

○ % of all electricity used that comes from nuclear power

USA
100.7

UK
10.1

CHINA
10.0

131.4 million babies

are born each year

360,000 births every day, 18,000 births every hour, 250 births every minute and four births every second.

ALCOHOL

LITRES OF PURE ALCOHOL
CONSUMED PER PERSON, 2005

▶ Alcohol consumption is the
cause of 2.5 million deaths a year
worldwide. This represents 4% of
total deaths worldwide each year,
a greater percentage than those
caused by Aids, tuberculosis
or violence.

MOLDOVA:
18.2

CZECH
REPUBLIC:
16.5

▶ Alcohol abuse is especially dangerous to men, with 6.2% of male deaths aged 15–59 attributable to alcohol, compared with 1.1% of female deaths. 11.5% of all drinkers worldwide admit to regular binge drinking.

▶ Average consumption worldwide was equal to 6.1 litres of pure alcohol per person aged over 15. Despite this, in 2005 half of all men and two thirds of all women worldwide had not had a drink in the last year.

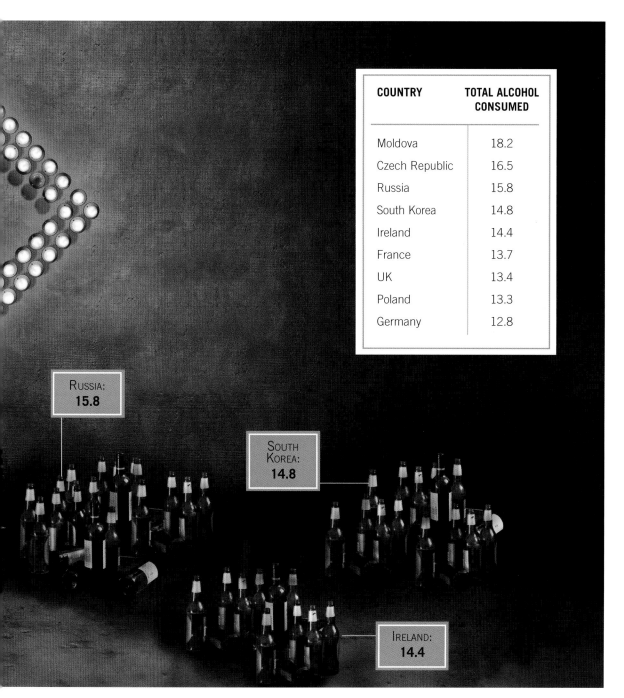

COUNTRY	TOTAL ALCOHOL CONSUMED
Moldova	18.2
Czech Republic	16.5
Russia	15.8
South Korea	14.8
Ireland	14.4
France	13.7
UK	13.4
Poland	13.3
Germany	12.8

RUSSIA: **15.8**

SOUTH KOREA: **14.8**

IRELAND: **14.4**

CORRUPTION

▶ Transparency International's Corruption Index is based on information provided by country experts, business leaders and independent institutions such as the World Bank and the World Economic Forum.

LEAST AND MOST CORRUPT NATIONS, 2010

LEAST

DENMARK
NEW ZEALAND
SINGAPORE
FINLAND
SWEDEN

		0	2	4	6	8	10
Denmark	9.3						
New Zealand	9.3						
Singapore	9.3						
Finland	9.2						
Sweden	9.2						
Canada	8.9						
Netherlands	8.8						
Australia	8.7						
Switzerland	8.7						
Norway	8.6						

N.B. The World Corruption Index measures perceptions of domestic and public sector corruption. Each country is ranked

▶ Outside the top ten were: 15 – Germany, 17 – Japan, 20 – UK, 22 – USA, 25 – France, 30 – Spain, 67 – Italy. Improvements in corruption scores between 2009 and 2010 were found in Bhutan, Chile, Ecuador, Haiti, Jamaica and Kuwait.

▶ In 2010 corruption worsened in: Czech Republic, Greece, Hungary, Italy, Niger and the USA. In 2010 nearly three quarters of all the 178 nations on the Corruption Index scored less than five, indicating high levels of corruption.

MOST
SOMALIA
BURMA
AFGHANISTAN
IRAQ UZBEKISTAN

| | 0 | 2 | 4 | 6 | 8 | 10 |

SOMALIA 1.1
BURMA 1.4
AFGHANISTAN 1.4
IRAQ 1.5
UZBEKISTAN 1.6
TURKMENISTAN 1.6
SUDAN 1.6
CHAD 1.7
BURUNDI 1.8
EQUATORIAL GUINEA 1.9

from zero to ten, with zero the highest level of corruption and ten the lowest

OBESITY

% OF ADULT POPULATION THAT IS OBESE, 2010

▶ People with a Body Mass Index (BMI) of more than 25 are classed as overweight, those 30 or over are classed as obese. Overweight people have a greater risk of diabetes and heart disease.

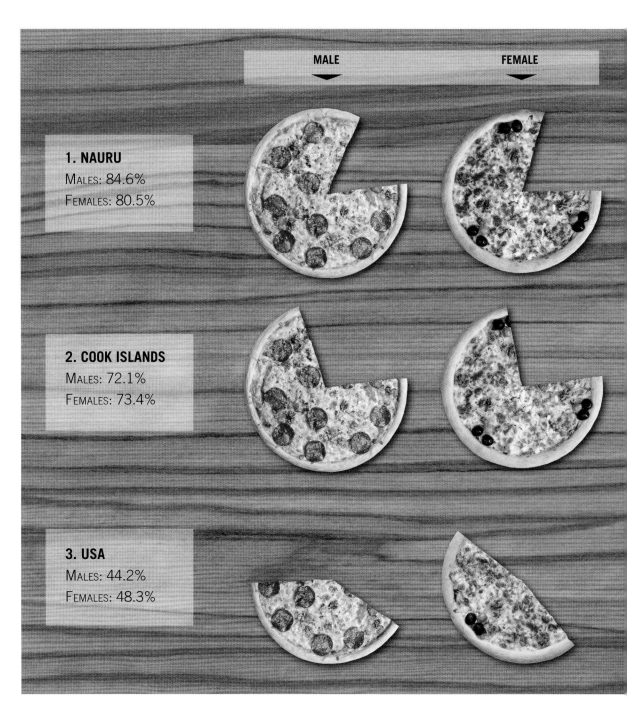

MALE **FEMALE**

1. NAURU
MALES: 84.6%
FEMALES: 80.5%

2. COOK ISLANDS
MALES: 72.1%
FEMALES: 73.4%

3. USA
MALES: 44.2%
FEMALES: 48.3%

According to the World Health Organization, in 2008 1.4 billion adults aged over 20 worldwide were overweight and 200 million men and nearly 300 million women were classed as obese.

Over 2.8 million adults die worldwide every year as a result of being overweight or obese. More people die each year from being overweight or obese than from being underweight.

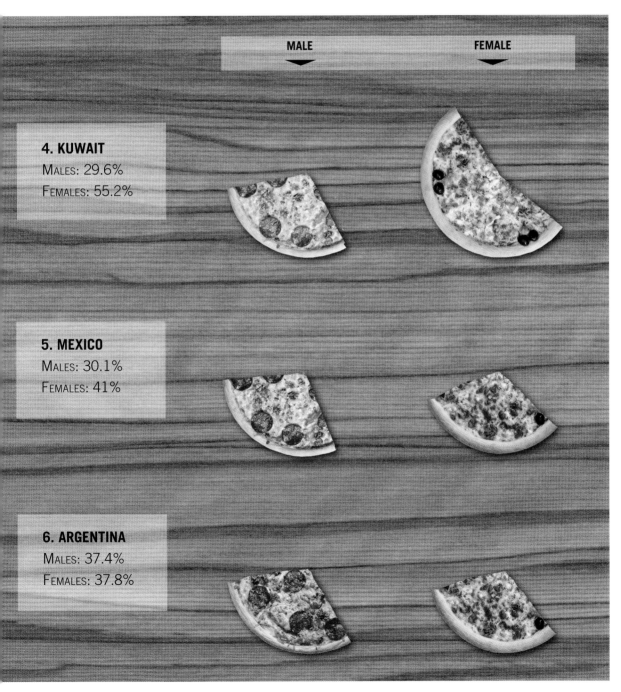

MALE

FEMALE

4. KUWAIT
MALES: 29.6%
FEMALES: 55.2%

5. MEXICO
MALES: 30.1%
FEMALES: 41%

6. ARGENTINA
MALES: 37.4%
FEMALES: 37.8%

RELIGION

% AFFILIATED WITH A RELIGION, 2011

▶ Christianity has the most followers worldwide, with an estimated 2 billion adherents. The USA has the largest Christian population in the world with approximately 224 million followers.

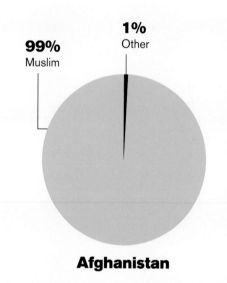

99%
Muslim

1%
Other

Afghanistan

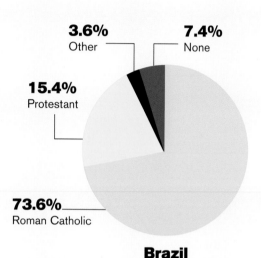

3.6%
Other

7.4%
None

15.4%
Protestant

73.6%
Roman Catholic

Brazil

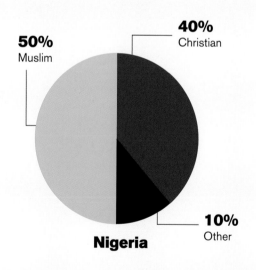

50%
Muslim

40%
Christian

10%
Other

Nigeria

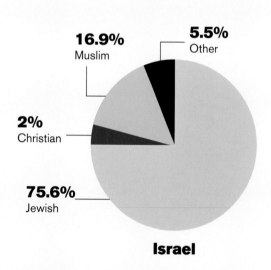

16.9%
Muslim

5.5%
Other

2%
Christian

75.6%
Jewish

Israel

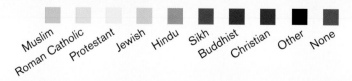

Muslim Roman Catholic Protestant Jewish Hindu Sikh Buddhist Christian Other None

▶ Islam is the second biggest religion with approximately 1.5 billion followers. Hinduism is the third with 900 million. Other large religions include: Buddhism 376m, Sikhism 23m, and Judaism 14m.

▶ Islam has been dubbed the fastest growing religion in the world because the largest populations of Muslims are in countries with high birth rates such as Indonesia, India and Egypt.

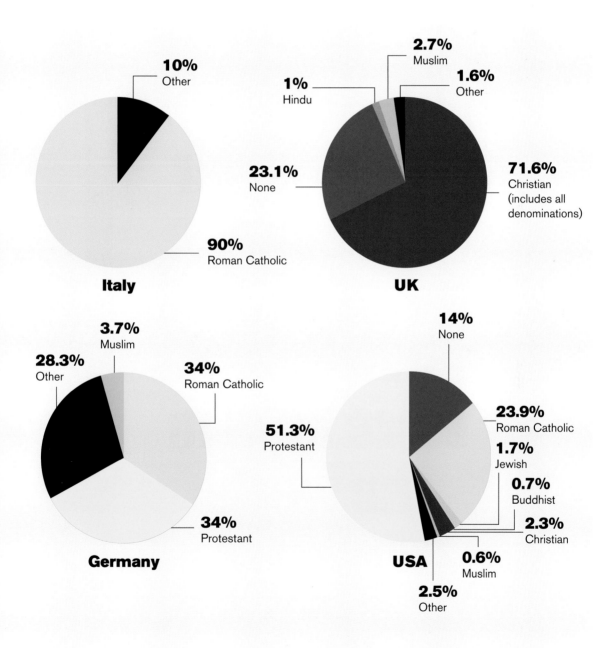

10%
Other

1%
Hindu

2.7%
Muslim

1.6%
Other

23.1%
None

71.6%
Christian
(includes all
denominations)

90%
Roman Catholic

Italy

UK

3.7%
Muslim

28.3%
Other

34%
Roman Catholic

51.3%
Protestant

34%
Protestant

Germany

14%
None

23.9%
Roman Catholic

1.7%
Jewish

0.7%
Buddhist

2.3%
Christian

2.5%
Other

0.6%
Muslim

USA

During the first quarter of 2012 Apple sold more iPhones per second

(4.6)

than babies were born in the world

(4.2 births per second)

The desire to keep up with the latest smart phone technology means that on average people replace their phones every two years or less.

NEWSPAPERS

% WHO CITE NEWSPAPERS AS
THEIR SOURCE OF NEWS, 2007

▶ The decline in sales of
newspapers has had a surprising
knock-on effect in the global
paper industry, which is now
struggling to find sources of high
quality paper for recycling.

> 50%

N.B. % of respondents who cite newspapers
as their first or second source for
national and international news.

INDIA
JAPAN
75%

VENEZUELA
73%

SWEDEN
66%

CHINA
63%

GERMANY
62%

UK
58%

SPAIN
57%

FRANCE
53%

ITALY
53%

▶ The world's largest selling newspaper Is the *Yomiuri Shimbun* from Japan with a combined circulation of its morning and evening editions of over 14 million copies.

▶ In 1605 the world's first newspaper *Relation aller Furnemmen und Gedenckwürdigen Historien* (Account of all distinguished and commemorable news) was published in Germany.

≤ **50%**

RUSSIA
50%

SOUTH AFRICA
TURKEY
49%

SOUTH KOREA
USA
47%

POLAND
45%

KENYA
41%

ARGENTINA
37%

NIGERIA
35%

MOROCCO
20%

OLD AGE

% AGED OVER 65 AND 80, 2008

▶ In 2008 there were 506 million people aged 65 or over, this represents 7% of the world's population. It is predicted that by 2018 people aged over 65 will outnumber people aged under five for the first time.

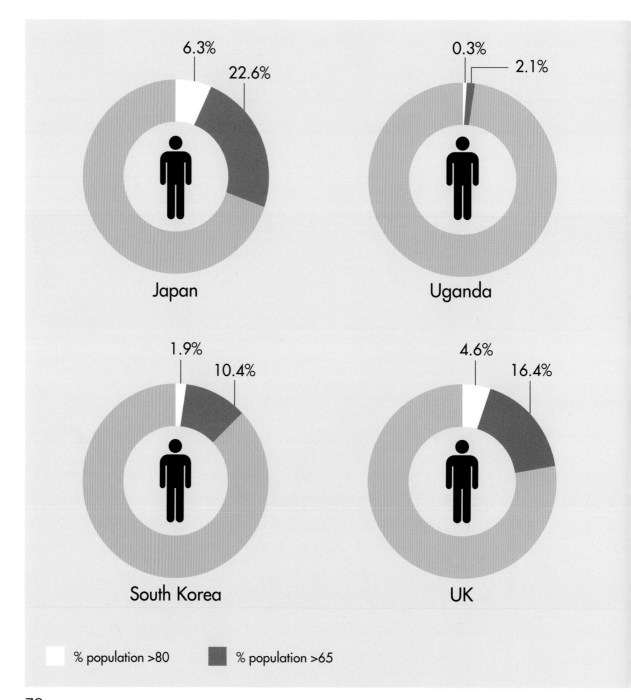

6.3%

22.6%

Japan

0.3%

2.1%

Uganda

1.9%

10.4%

South Korea

4.6%

16.4%

UK

☐ % population >80   ■ % population >65

▶ The rapidly ageing population will have huge implications on all societies, with the greater need for healthcare, pensions and long-term care putting huge pressure on the younger workforce to pay for such measures.

▶ It is forecast that by 2050 the world's population aged 60 and over will reach 2 billion. People aged 60 years and older are the world's fastest growing age group. Europe has the largest ageing population.

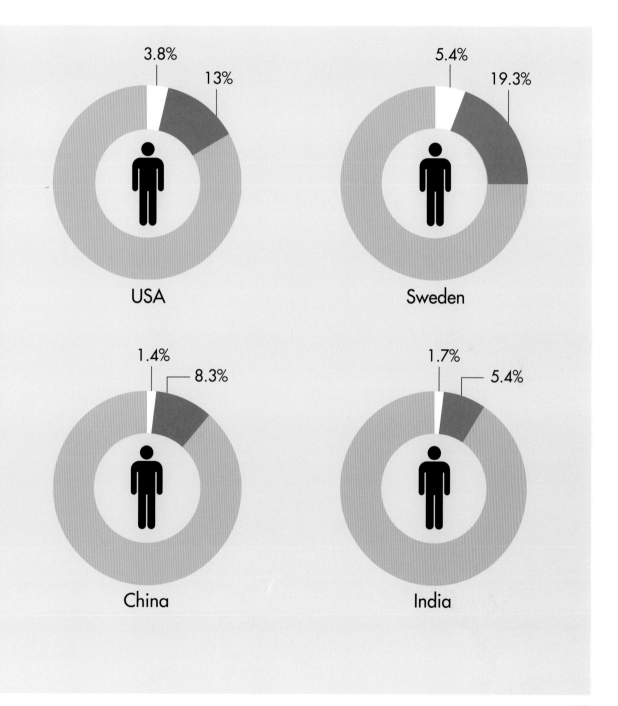

3.8%   13%

USA

5.4%   19.3%

Sweden

1.4%   8.3%

China

1.7%   5.4%

India

POPULATION

TOP TEN COUNTRIES 2011
AND 2050 (ESTIMATED)

▶ Niger has the youngest
population with 48.9% under
fifteen. Monaco is the most
densely populated country
with 16,923 people crammed
into every square kilometre.

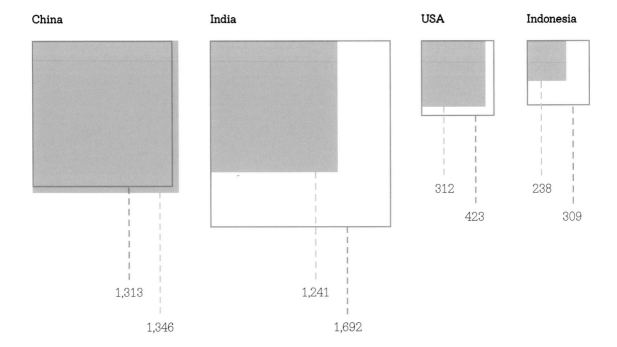

China
1,313
1,346

India
1,241
1,692

USA
312
423

Indonesia
238
309

- The Pacific state of Niue is one of the least populous countries in the world with just 1,400 residents – such is the small size of the country that each of its MPs represents just 30 people.

- The United Nations Population Division estimated that it took until about 1800 for the world population to reach 1 billion and a further 130 years until 1930 for the world population to reach 2 billion.

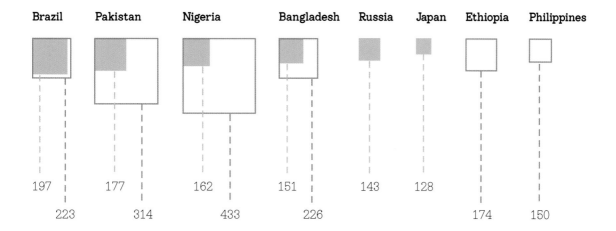

| Brazil | Pakistan | Nigeria | Bangladesh | Russia | Japan | Ethiopia | Philippines |

| 197 | 177 | 162 | 151 | 143 | 128 | | |
| 223 | 314 | 433 | 226 | | | 174 | 150 |

Population 2011 (millions)

Population 2050 est. (millions)

IN 2011 THERE WERE

12

MAJOR ONGOING WORLD CONFLICTS

The United Nations defines a major world conflict as one that results in more than 1,000 battlefield deaths a year.

THE MOST VIOLENT OF THESE CONFLICTS IS THE ONGOING WAR AGAINST DRUGS CARTELS IN MEXICO – SINCE 2006 OVER

50,000

HAVE LOST THEIR LIVES

FORESTS

COVERAGE IN SQUARE
KILOMETRES

▶ Forests cover about 22% of the planet. The majority are in three swathes – the Canadian and Alaskan boreal forest, the boreal forest of Russia, and the Amazon Basin and Guyana Shield.

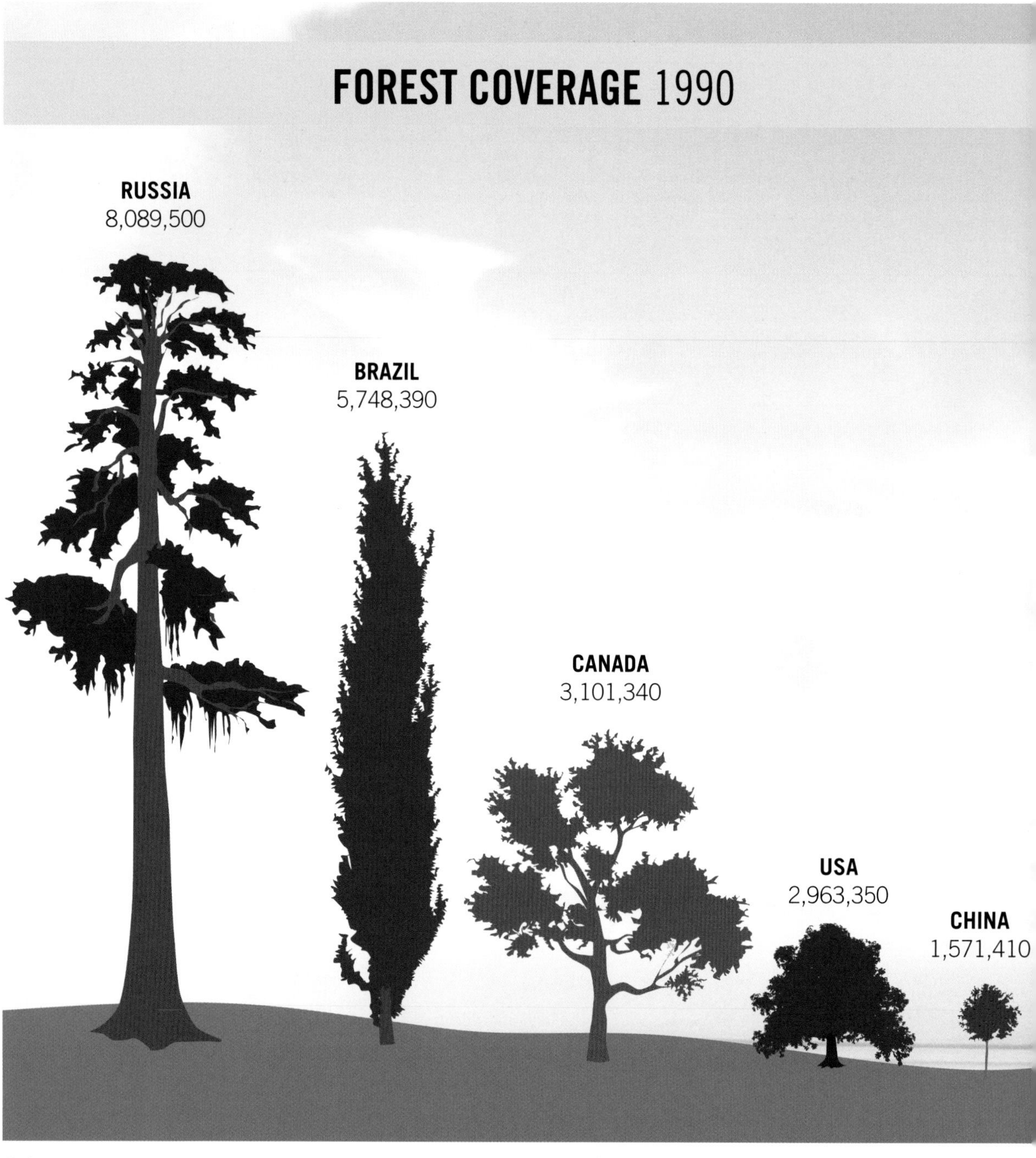

FOREST COVERAGE 1990

RUSSIA
8,089,500

BRAZIL
5,748,390

CANADA
3,101,340

USA
2,963,350

CHINA
1,571,410

▶ Historically forests covered almost all of Europe, three-quarters of Canada and nearly half of the USA. Each year an estimated 16 million hectares of forest are lost to deforestation.

▶ In Europe and North America deforestation has largely stabilized as the majority of their forests were cleared centuries ago. In contrast, deforestation in South America, Africa and Asia continues apace.

FOREST COVERAGE 2010

RUSSIA
8,090,900

BRAZIL
5,195,220

CANADA
3,101,340

USA
3,040,220

CHINA
2,068,610

BIRTH RATE

ANNUAL BIRTH RATE
PER 1000, 2011

▶ The population replacement rate
(meaning the number of births
needed to keep a population at
a stable level by replacing those
who die) has been calculated
as 2.1 babies per woman.

N.B. The birth rate relates to
the crude birth rate – the
number of babies born during
a year per 1,000 people.

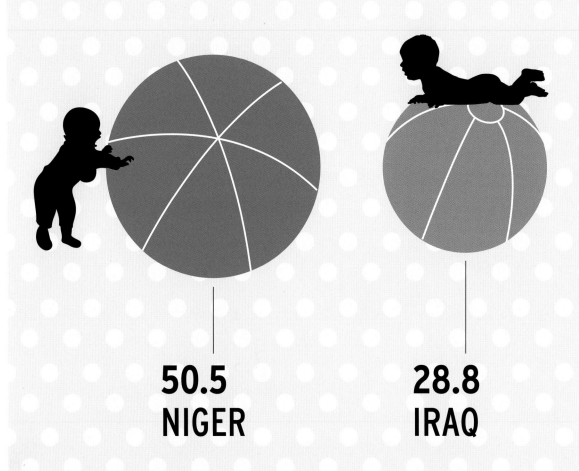

50.5
NIGER

28.8
IRAQ

▶ Over 70 countries have a fertility rate of 2.1 or less. Family size and family wealth show a strong correlation, with richer familes (and countries) tending to have lower fertility levels than poorer families.

▶ The Japanese Government has introduced incentives to encourage childbirth such as daycare schemes and benefits for working mothers but the birth rate has remained one of the lowest in the world.

20.9
INDIA

16.1
IRELAND

12.3
UK

10
POLAND

7.3
JAPAN

HIV

% OF POPULATION WITH HIV
(15–49 YEARS OLD), 2007

▶ 34 million people were living with HIV in 2010 – that breaks down to 30.1 million adults, 16.8 million women and 3.4 million children under 15. 67% of all people living with HIV reside in Africa.

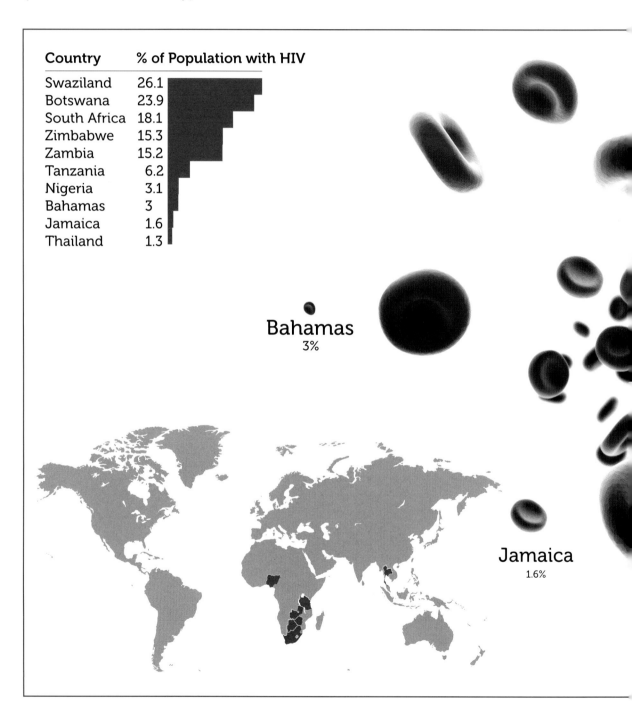

Country	% of Population with HIV
Swaziland	26.1
Botswana	23.9
South Africa	18.1
Zimbabwe	15.3
Zambia	15.2
Tanzania	6.2
Nigeria	3.1
Bahamas	3
Jamaica	1.6
Thailand	1.3

Bahamas
3%

Jamaica
1.6%

- 1.8 million people (1.5 million adults and 250,000 children) died from Aids in 2010. HIV and Aids have resulted in 16.6 million children aged 0–17 worldwide losing their parents.

- Aid work to encourage condom use and improve access to antiretroviral drugs has helped to bring down the rate of new infections from 3 million in 2001 to 2.7 million in 2007.

Thailand
1.3%

Zimbabwe
15.3%

Swaziland
26.1%

South
Africa
18.1%

Botswana
23.9%

MOBILE PHONES

NUMBER OF MOBILE PHONE
SUBSCRIBERS, 2010

▶ By 2010 90% of the world was
covered by mobile phone networks.
Smartphones (such as the iPhone)
represent just 13% of all mobile
handsets globally and yet account
for 78% of global handset traffic.

RUSSIA
238,000,000

IRAN
67,500,000

CHINA
859,000,000

INDIA
752,000,000

INDONESIA
238,000,000

FRANCE
64,000,000

- 48 million people worldwide own a mobile phone and yet do not have electricity at home, according to Cisco. Nokia is the world's biggest mobile phone manufacturer, selling 3.4 billion handsets since 1994.

- A report by consultants Wireless Intelligence in 2010 suggested there were now 5 billion mobile phones worldwide, which is three times more mobile phones worldwide than personal computers.

USA
279,000,999

BANGLADESH
68,650,000

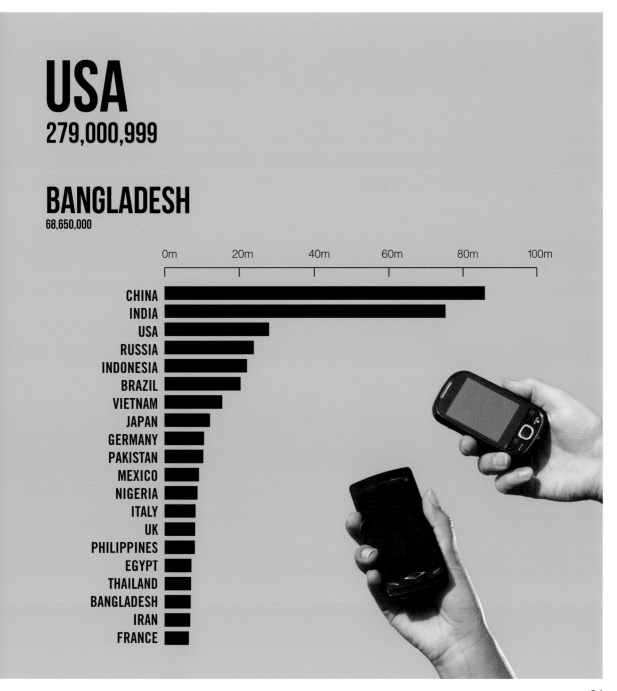

	0m	20m	40m	60m	80m	100m
CHINA						
INDIA						
USA						
RUSSIA						
INDONESIA						
BRAZIL						
VIETNAM						
JAPAN						
GERMANY						
PAKISTAN						
MEXICO						
NIGERIA						
ITALY						
UK						
PHILIPPINES						
EGYPT						
THAILAND						
BANGLADESH						
IRAN						
FRANCE						

70%
of the world's surface is covered in water,

97.5%
of all water on earth is salt water.

Of the

2.5%

of fresh water on earth, nearly

70%

of it is held in frozen ice caps.

This means that globally less than

1%

of fresh water is found in accessible lakes, reservoirs and streams.

ARMS

TOP TEN SUPPLIERS AND
RECIPIENTS OF ARMS

▶ The USA is the biggest supplier
of weapons: in 2008 it was
responsible for 68.4% of all arms
deals. The developing world is the
primary focus for most weapons
suppliers. The top buyers in 2008
were the UAE.

ARMS SUPPLIERS – value of arms deals, 2001-2008 ($US millions)

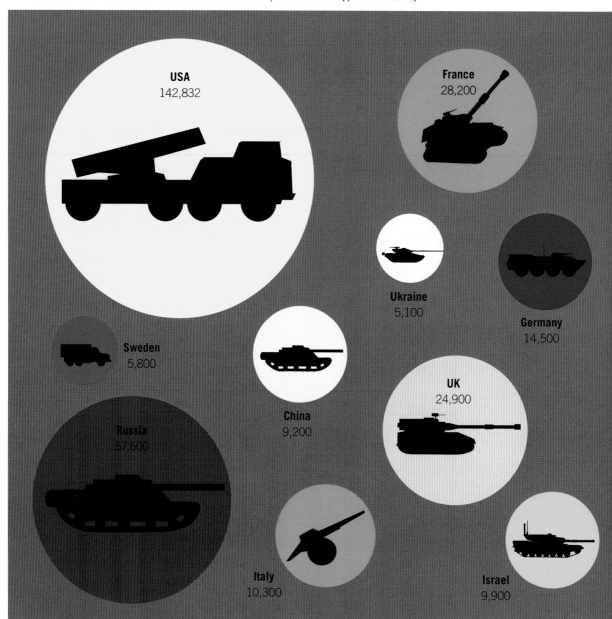

USA
142,832

France
28,200

Ukraine
5,100

Germany
14,500

Sweden
5,800

China
9,200

UK
24,900

Russia
57,600

Italy
10,300

Israel
9,900

▶ The largest individual arms dealer in 2010 was British company BAE, which took in weapons orders worth £21 billion.The USA spends the most on military expenditure, accounting for 54% of the world's military spending.

▶ 30% of orders from the USA in the last five years were for combat aircraft. Since 2008 countries in Latin America, Africa and Asia have increased their military spending. Most European countries have cut budgets.

RECIPIENTS OF ARMS DEALS – % of total arms sales, 2006-2010

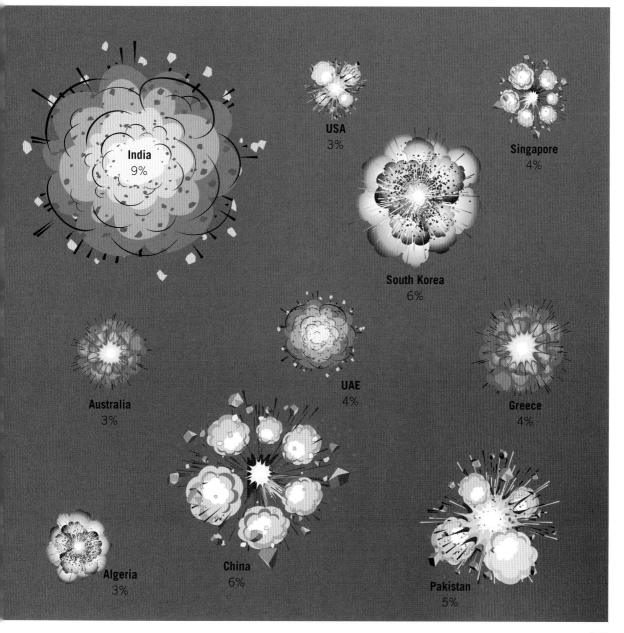

India
9%

USA
3%

Singapore
4%

South Korea
6%

Australia
3%

UAE
4%

Greece
4%

Algeria
3%

China
6%

Pakistan
5%

OIL RESERVES

CRUDE OIL RESERVES IN BARRELS, 2011

▶ The cost of crude oil hit an all time high of $147 a barrel in July 2008. Most crude oil fields have passed their peak of production resulting in a sharp decline in oil production, which in turn causes higher and higher oil prices.

AZERBAIJAN
7,000,000,000

CANADA
175,200,000,000

SAUDI ARABIA
262,600,000,000

ECUADOR
6,510,000,000

VENEZUELA
211,200,000,000

▶ Many of the largest oil fields remain untapped due to the difficulty of extraction. A reserve off the coast of Brazil is estimated to contain 33 billion barrels. It lies under 5,000 feet of water and 25,000 feet of sea floor, so extraction is unlikely.

▶ The world's worst oil spill occurred in 1991 when Iraqi soldiers deliberately opened oil valves and emptied an estimated 10.3 million barrels of oil into Kuwait's Sea Island terminal, with the intention of preventing US marines landing.

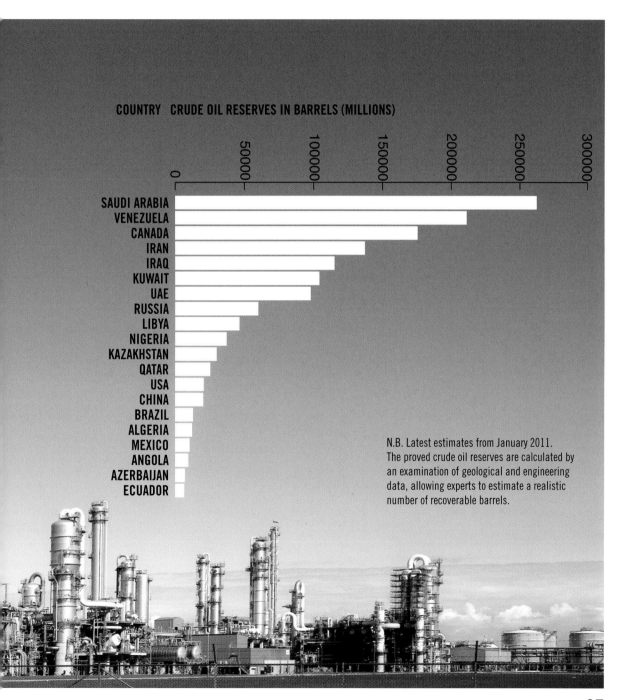

COUNTRY CRUDE OIL RESERVES IN BARRELS (MILLIONS)

0	
50000	
100000	
150000	
200000	
250000	
300000	

SAUDI ARABIA
VENEZUELA
CANADA
IRAN
IRAQ
KUWAIT
UAE
RUSSIA
LIBYA
NIGERIA
KAZAKHSTAN
QATAR
USA
CHINA
BRAZIL
ALGERIA
MEXICO
ANGOLA
AZERBAIJAN
ECUADOR

N.B. Latest estimates from January 2011. The proved crude oil reserves are calculated by an examination of geological and engineering data, allowing experts to estimate a realistic number of recoverable barrels.

WATER

LITRES OF BOTTLED WATER
PER PERSON ANNUALLY, 2010

▶ Bottled water generally costs consumers a thousand times more per litre than good quality municipal tap water. In the USA almost 50% of all bottled water sold is repackaged tap water.

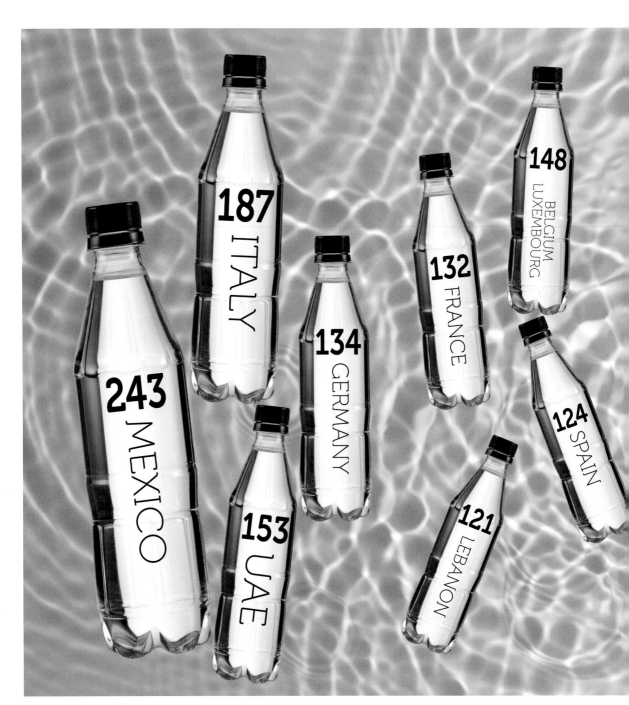

187 ITALY

148 BELGIUM LUXEMBOURG

132 FRANCE

134 GERMANY

243 MEXICO

153 UAE

124 SPAIN

121 LEBANON

It is predicted that in 2012 the world's consumption of bottled water will reach 272 billion litres. Worldwide, still water is far more popular than sparkling, accounting for 86% of all bottled water sales.

An estimated 17 million barrels of oil are used in the production of plastic water bottles every year and it takes three times the amount of water to manufacture a plastic water bottle as it does to fill it.

114 THAILAND

111 HUNGARY

108 SWITZERLAND

107 USA

107 SLOVENIA

101 CROATIA

98 CYPRUS

95 QATAR

95 SAUDI ARABIA

95 CHINA

92 CZECH REPUBLIC

91 AUSTRIA

There were

22,289

earthquakes recorded worldwide by the US Geological Survey in 2011.

The majority of these (13,315) measured between

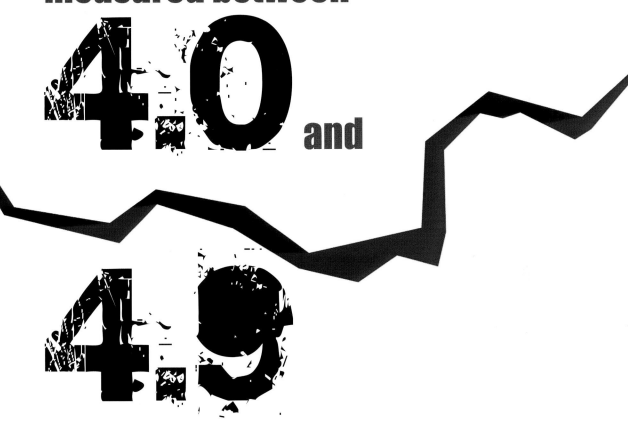

4.0 and

4.9

on the Richter scale.

DRUG USE

CANNABIS AND COCAINE
USE, 2008

▶ Despite cannabis use being legal
in the Netherlands a relatively low
(19.8%) number of adults admit ever
using the drug. Up to 203 million
people have used cannabis, making
it the most widely taken drug.

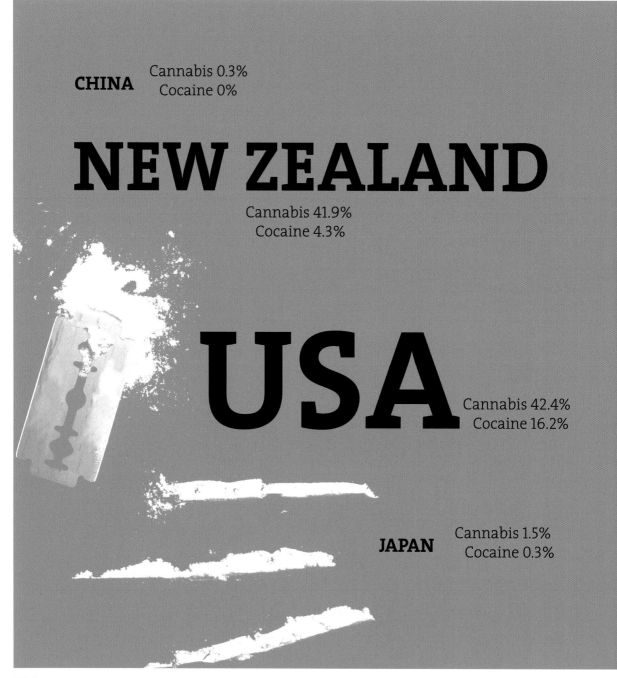

CHINA Cannabis 0.3%
Cocaine 0%

NEW ZEALAND

Cannabis 41.9%
Cocaine 4.3%

USA
Cannabis 42.4%
Cocaine 16.2%

JAPAN Cannabis 1.5%
Cocaine 0.3%

▶ Cannabis use can often begin at a young age, with 20% of 15-year-olds and 54% of 21-year-olds in the USA admitting to trying the drug. In contrast, very few 15-year-olds around the world have tried cocaine.

▶ The median age worldwide for first trying cannabis is 16 to 19 years old whereas for trying cocaine it is 21 to 24 years old. Children who have a high IQ are more likely to go on to take drugs in later life.

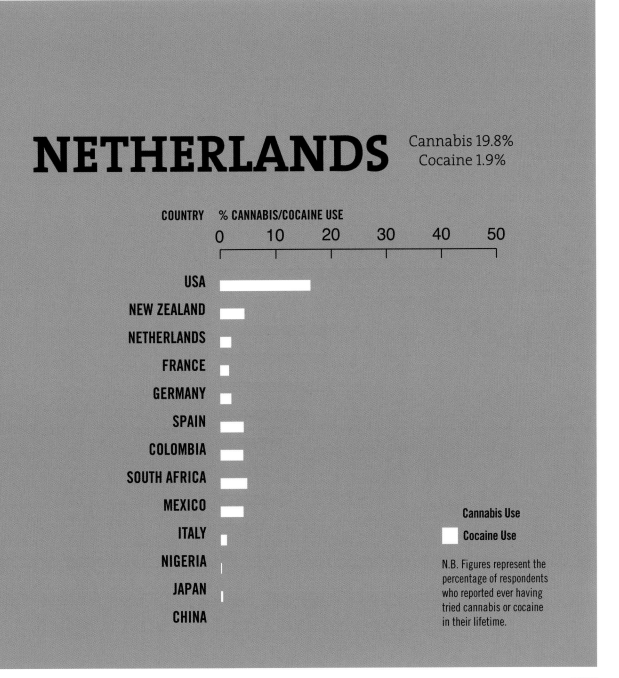

NETHERLANDS

Cannabis 19.8%
Cocaine 1.9%

COUNTRY	% CANNABIS/COCAINE USE

USA
NEW ZEALAND
NETHERLANDS
FRANCE
GERMANY
SPAIN
COLOMBIA
SOUTH AFRICA
MEXICO
ITALY
NIGERIA
JAPAN
CHINA

Cannabis Use
Cocaine Use

N.B. Figures represent the percentage of respondents who reported ever having tried cannabis or cocaine in their lifetime.

OLYMPICS

COUNTRIES THAT HAVE
HOSTED OLYMPIC GAMES, 2012

▶ In 2012 London became the first city to host the summer games three times. Host countries are mainly clustered in the northern hemisphere – an African nation has never hosted an Olympic Games.

SUMMER

USA
4

UK
3

Germany
2

Greece
2

Australia
2

France
2

Europe has hosted the most games with 30, followed by North America with 12, Asia with 5 and Oceania with 2. The summer Olympic Games were cancelled due to war in 1916, 1940 and 1944.

Host cities are selected seven years before the games and face an inspection by International Olympic Committee evaluation teams before a vote of all IOC members decides the winner.

WINTER

USA
4

France
3

Japan
2

Switzerland
2

Italy
2

Canada
2

Norway
2

Austria
2

PEACE

MOST AND LEAST PEACEFUL
NATIONS, 2011

▶ Outside the top ten list of the most peaceful nations in the world we find Sweden at 13, Germany at 15, Australia at 18, Poland at 22, UK at 26, Italy at 45, China at 80 and the USA at 82.

MOST PEACEFUL RANK 2011

ICELAND
NEW ZEALAND
JAPAN
DENMARK
CZECH REPUBLIC
AUSTRIA
FINLAND
CANADA
NORWAY
SLOVENIA

N.B. The index is created using 23 indicators, such as relationship with neighbouring countries, human rights record, and military expenditure.

▶ It is estimated that if all violence had ceased in 2010 the world would have saved $8.12 trillion. 40% of the world's least peaceful nations are found in sub-Saharan Africa, such as Somalia and Sudan.

▶ The likelihood of terrorist attacks increased in 29 countries in 2011. Between 2010 and 2011 Libya saw the greatest drop down the peace rankings, going from 56 in 2010 to 143 in 2011.

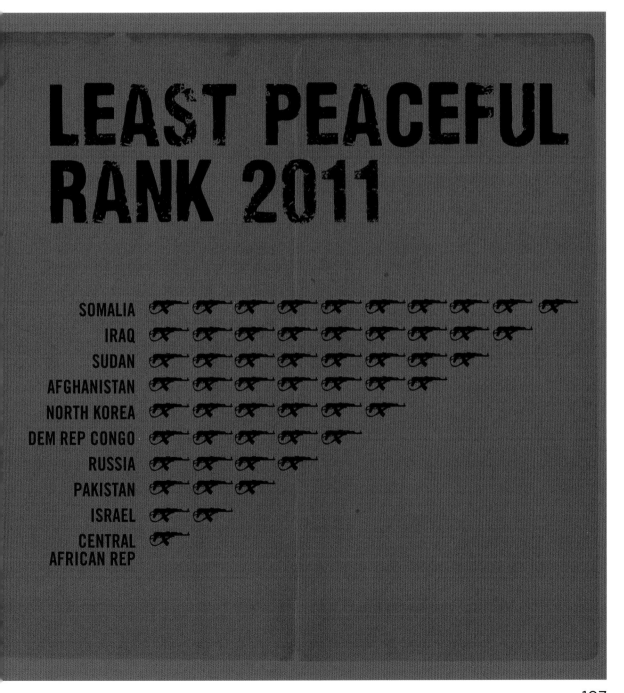

LEAST PEACEFUL RANK 2011

SOMALIA

IRAQ

SUDAN

AFGHANISTAN

NORTH KOREA

DEM REP CONGO

RUSSIA

PAKISTAN

ISRAEL

CENTRAL AFRICAN REP

SATISFACTION

SELF-REPORTED LIFE
SATISFACTION (OUT OF 10), 2007

▶ Between 1981 and 2007 researchers noted that in 45 out of 52 countries levels of happiness increased. It is believed greater social tolerance and economic development have led to a perception of greater personal freedom.

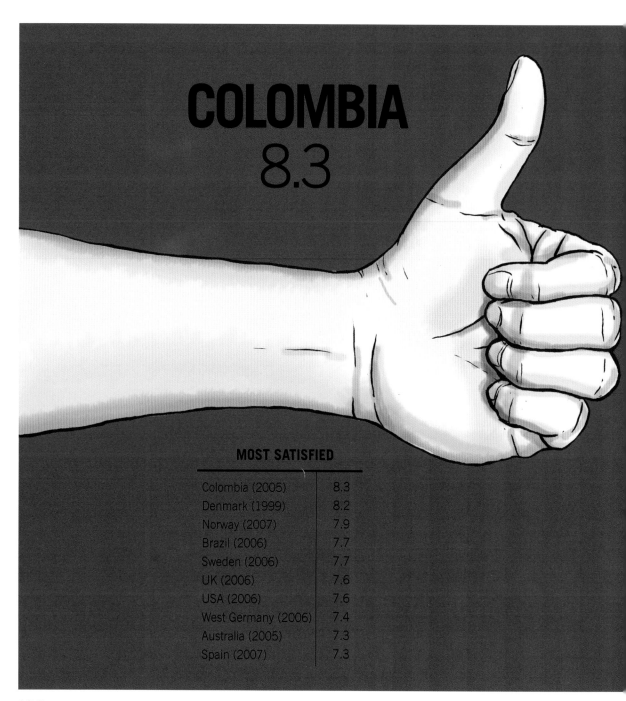

COLOMBIA
8.3

MOST SATISFIED

Colombia (2005)	8.3
Denmark (1999)	8.2
Norway (2007)	7.9
Brazil (2006)	7.7
Sweden (2006)	7.7
UK (2006)	7.6
USA (2006)	7.6
West Germany (2006)	7.4
Australia (2005)	7.3
Spain (2007)	7.3

▶ In October 2011 research suggested that the happiest people have a 35% lower risk of death than the least happy. The same year it was found that only 35% of people in Hungary, Estonia and Turkey were satisfied with their lives.

▶ Middle-aged people around the world are the least happy age group according to research in 2010. However being married and having children are factors that generally produce greater life satisfaction.

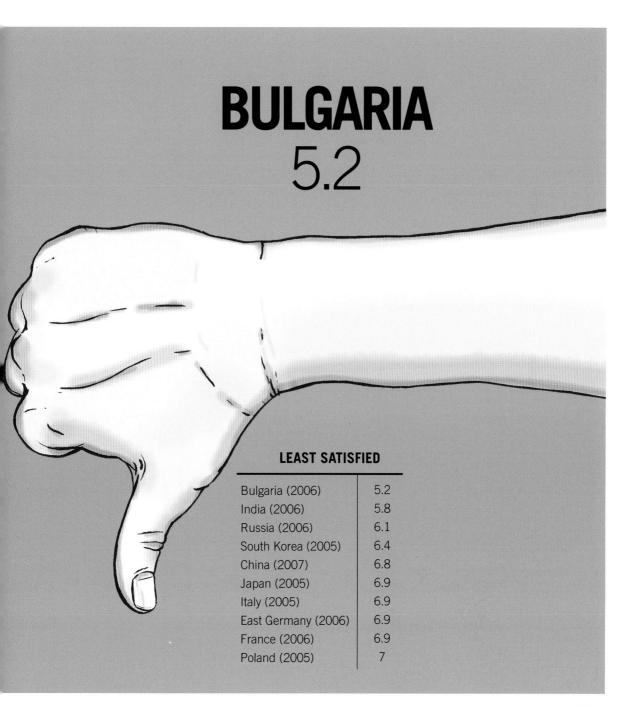

BULGARIA
5.2

LEAST SATISFIED

Bulgaria (2006)	5.2
India (2006)	5.8
Russia (2006)	6.1
South Korea (2005)	6.4
China (2007)	6.8
Japan (2005)	6.9
Italy (2005)	6.9
East Germany (2006)	6.9
France (2006)	6.9
Poland (2005)	7

CO$_2$

METRIC TONNES PER
CAPITA, 2009

▶ Carbon dioxide emissions are primarily caused by the burning of fossil fuels and the manufacture of cement. The whole world emits 4.5 tonnes of carbon dioxide per person every year.

16.2
Canada

17.7
USA

3.9
Mexico

This data set examines carbon dioxide emitted per capita, which means that some of the smallest nations (such as Gibraltar) emit the greatest amount of CO$_2$ per person.

▸ If you look at total amounts emitted then China is the biggest producer, with 7,710 million tonnes (in 2009). The USA follows with 5,424, then India with 1,602, Russia with 1,572 and Japan with 1,097.

▸ China's carbon dioxide emissions have increased 171% since the year 2000. Worldwide between 2008 and 2009 Ukraine saw the biggest decrease in carbon dioxide emissions with a drop of 28%.

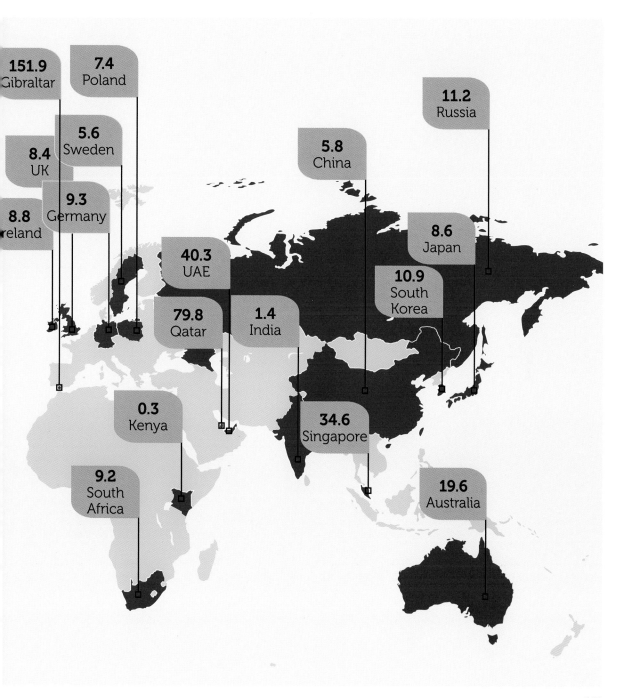

Value	Country
151.9	Gibraltar
7.4	Poland
11.2	Russia
5.6	Sweden
8.4	UK
5.8	China
9.3	Germany
8.6	Japan
8.8	Ireland
40.3	UAE
10.9	South Korea
79.8	Qatar
1.4	India
0.3	Kenya
34.6	Singapore
9.2	South Africa
19.6	Australia

ONLINE DATING

% RELATIONSHIPS THAT STARTED ONLINE SINCE 1997

▶ For those couples who did not meet their partner online, the most popular place to find a partner was: work (20%); bar, pub or club (19%); or through friends (16%) according to 2011 research by academics at the Oxford Internet Institute.

GERMANY
29%

BRAZIL
22.5%

UK
22.6%

NETHERLANDS
26.1%

FRANCE
26.1%

▶ Of those respondents in all countries who met their partner online, the most popular method was: on an online dating site (39%), followed by a chat room (24%) and through a social networking site (14%).

▶ Brazilians were most likely to use a social networking site to find a partner (38%), whereas Norwegians were more likely to use a traditional online dating site (64%). Brazilians are also the most frequent users of online dating.

55.3 MILLION PEOPLE DIE WORLDWIDE EACH YEAR

151,600
DEATHS EVERY DAY,
6,316
DEATHS EVERY HOUR,
105
PEOPLE DIE EVERY MINUTE
AND TWO PEOPLE DIE EVERY SECOND.

WOMEN IN POWER

% OF WOMEN IN
PARLIAMENT, 2011

▶ Worldwide, the global average
proportion of women occupying
seats in parliament is 19.3%.
Regionally, Nordic countries
have the highest proportion
of women in parliament
with an average of 42.1%.

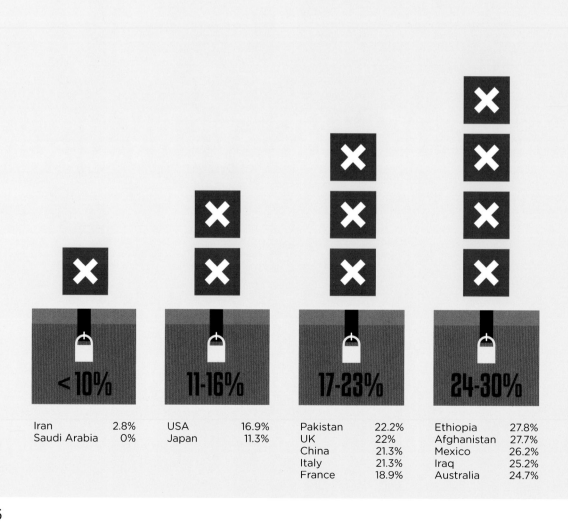

<10%		**11-16%**		**17-23%**		**24-30%**	
Iran	2.8%	USA	16.9%	Pakistan	22.2%	Ethiopia	27.8%
Saudi Arabia	0%	Japan	11.3%	UK	22%	Afghanistan	27.7%
				China	21.3%	Mexico	26.2%
				Italy	21.3%	Iraq	25.2%
				France	18.9%	Australia	24.7%

▶ In August 2011 there were 20 female Presidents or Prime Ministers worldwide. The first country to have a female Prime Minister was Sri Lanka which elected Sirimavo Bandaranaike in 1960.

▶ The first country to have a female President was Argentina when Isabel Peron suceeded her husband Juan after his death in office in 1974. Between 1994 and 2000 Sri Lanka had both a female Prime Minister and a female President.

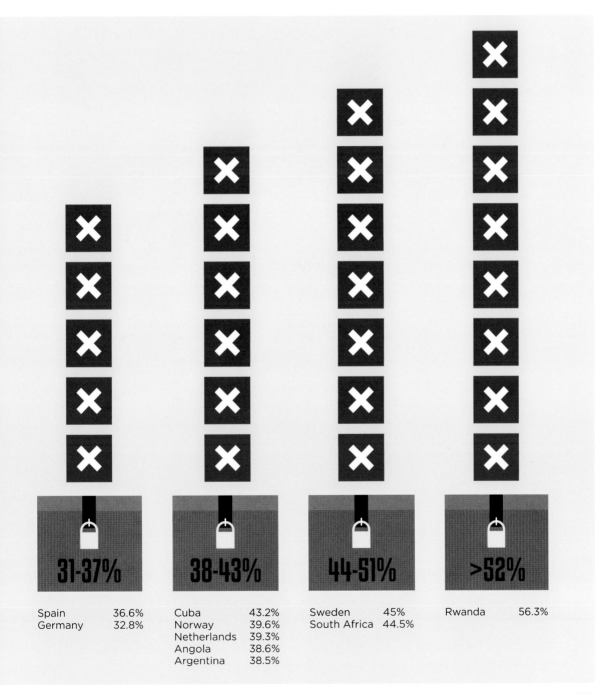

31-37%

Spain	36.6%
Germany	32.8%

38-43%

Cuba	43.2%
Norway	39.6%
Netherlands	39.3%
Angola	38.6%
Argentina	38.5%

44-51%

Sweden	45%
South Africa	44.5%

>52%

Rwanda	56.3%

REFUGEES

HOST AND SOURCE
NATIONS, 2010

▶ In 2010 there were 10.5 million refugees worldwide, an increase of 153,000 since 2009, largely because of the numbers fleeing Somalia. In 2010 an estimated 2.9 million Internally Displaced People were able to return home.

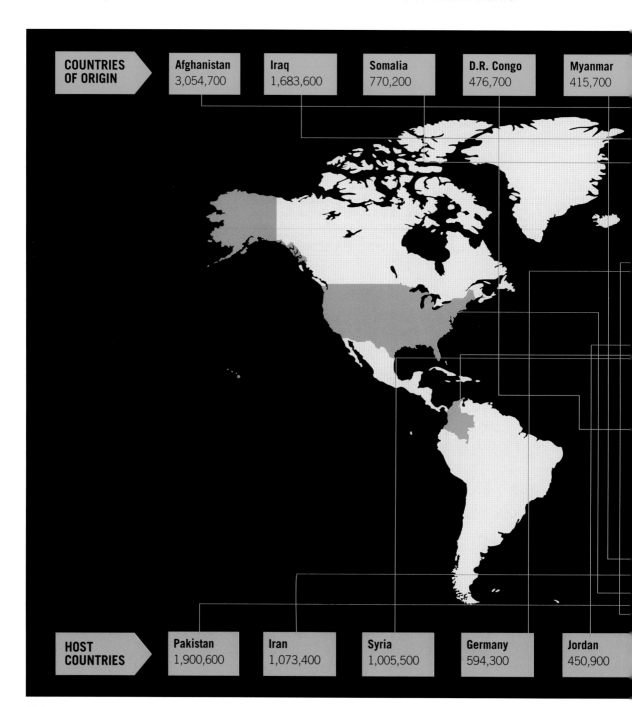

| COUNTRIES OF ORIGIN | Afghanistan 3,054,700 | Iraq 1,683,600 | Somalia 770,200 | D.R. Congo 476,700 | Myanmar 415,700 |

| HOST COUNTRIES | Pakistan 1,900,600 | Iran 1,073,400 | Syria 1,005,500 | Germany 594,300 | Jordan 450,900 |

► Only an estimated 17% of refugees leave their region of origin – most seek refuge in their neighbouring countries. The world's largest refugee camp is in Dadaab, Kenya – home to nearly 400,000 displaced Somalis.

► At the end of 2010 Asia Pacific was hosting the most refugees with 4 million, followed by Africa with 2.1 million, the Middle East and North Africa with 1.9 million, Europe with 1.6 million and the Americas with 800,000.

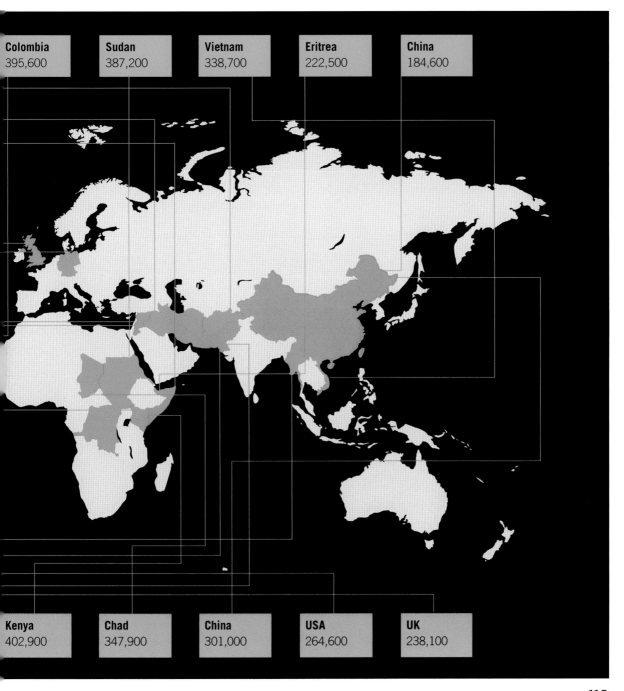

Colombia
395,600

Sudan
387,200

Vietnam
338,700

Eritrea
222,500

China
184,600

Kenya
402,900

Chad
347,900

China
301,000

USA
264,600

UK
238,100

ONLINE NEWS

SITED AS PRIMARY
NEWS SOURCE, 2007

▶ CNN.com is the most popular website for international news, so whilst online news is growing it is often consumed on websites run by traditional media companies.

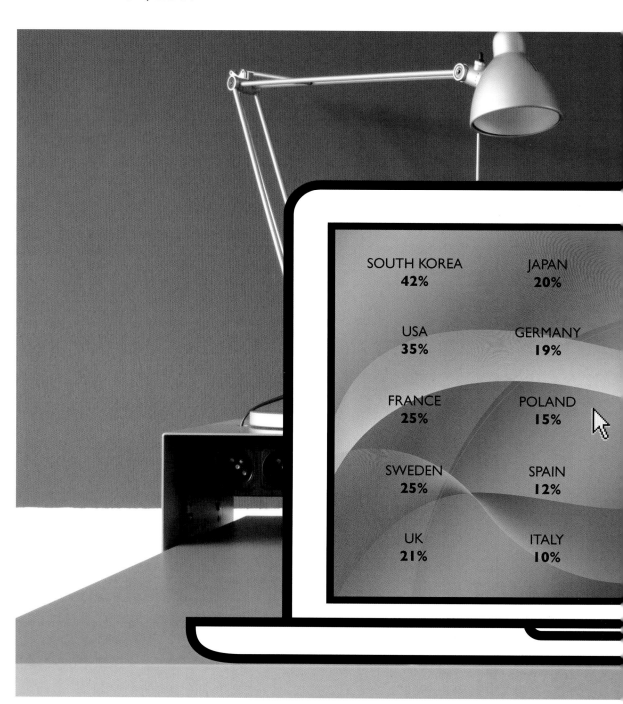

SOUTH KOREA	JAPAN
42%	20%
USA	GERMANY
35%	19%
FRANCE	POLAND
25%	15%
SWEDEN	SPAIN
25%	12%
UK	ITALY
21%	10%

▶ News is also consumed via sites such as YouTube, Facebook and Twitter. Al Jazeera videos on YouTube generate 2.5 million views per month.

▶ The most popular newspaper website is the UK's *Daily Mail*, visited by 45.3 million visitors each month. Second most popular is the *New York Times* with 44.8 million.

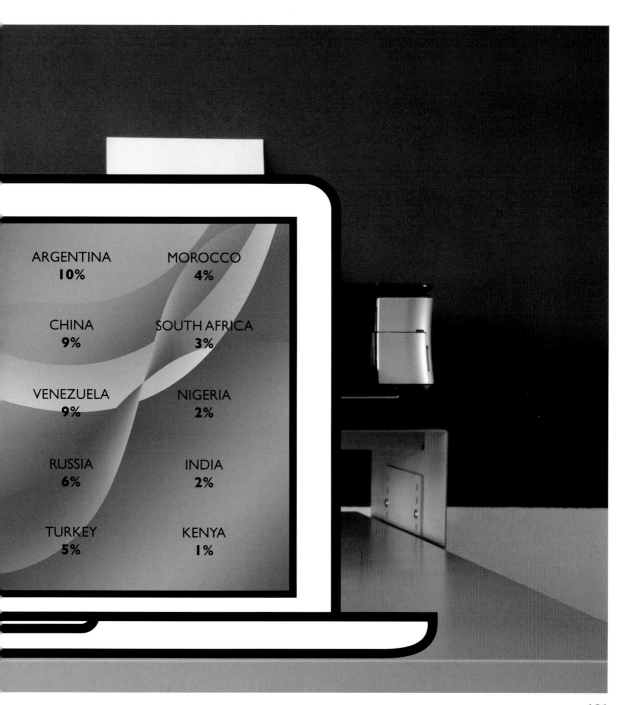

ARGENTINA
10%

MOROCCO
4%

CHINA
9%

SOUTH AFRICA
3%

VENEZUELA
9%

NIGERIA
2%

RUSSIA
6%

INDIA
2%

TURKEY
5%

KENYA
1%

TEENAGE PREGNANCY

NUMBERS PER 1,000 GIRLS
AGED 15 TO 19, 2010

▶ An estimated 16 million girls aged 15–19 give birth every year. 95% of these births are in developing countries. In Africa, the average adolescent fertility rate is 118, compared to 23 in Europe.

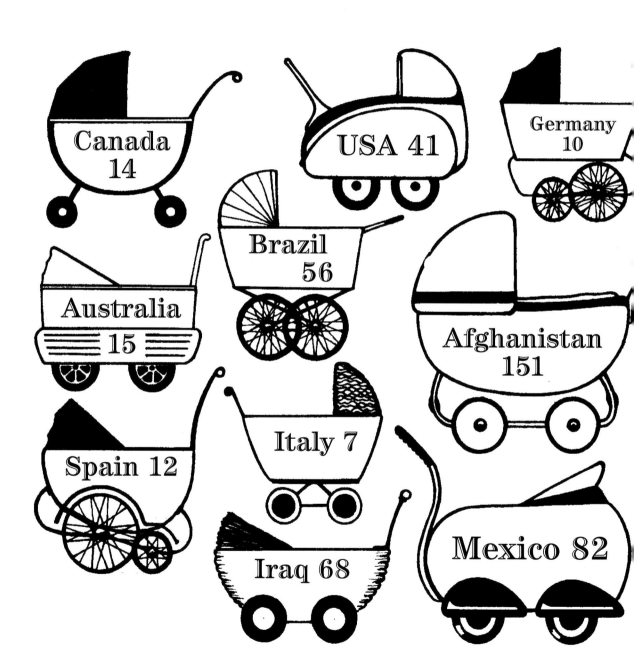

Canada 14

USA 41

Germany 10

Brazil 56

Australia 15

Afghanistan 151

Spain 12

Italy 7

Iraq 68

Mexico 82

▶ Mothers aged 15–19 face a far greater health risk than those over the age of 20. An average of 70,000 women aged 15–19 die during childbirth each year. Most of these are in developing countries.

▶ In the developed world teenage pregnancy is generally unplanned and occurs outside marriage; and a reported 82% of new mothers aged 15 or younger are also the daughters of teenage mothers.

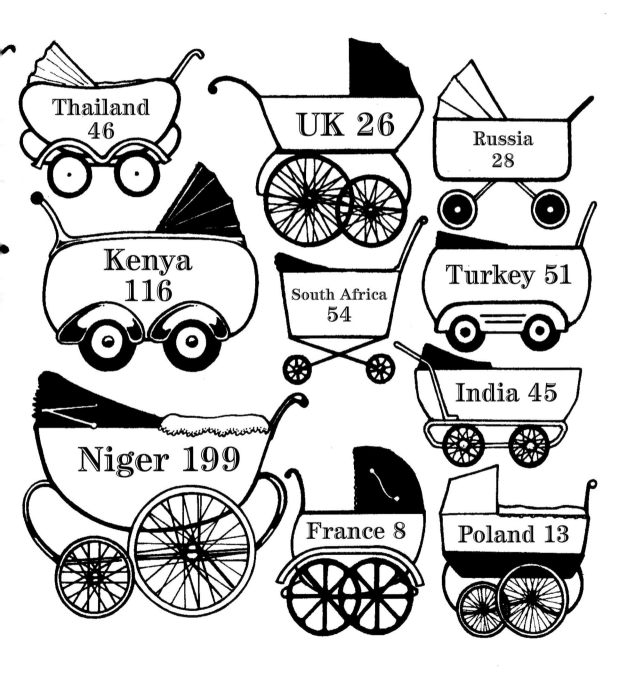

Thailand 46

UK 26

Russia 28

Kenya 116

South Africa 54

Turkey 51

India 45

Niger 199

France 8

Poland 13

Global life expectancy at birth is

67

YEARS OF AGE

26% of the global population

(1.8bn)

are under the age of 15

66% (4.4bn)

ARE AGED **15–64**

---

and **8%** **(516m)**

of the world's population are aged **over 65**

HAPPINESS

% HAPPY OR UNHAPPY, 2011

▶ Across the globe, the average % of respondents stating that they are happy is 53%, with only 13% saying they are unhappy. An average of 31% say that they are neither happy nor unhappy.

THE 5 HAPPIEST

	HAPPY	UNHAPPY
Fiji	89	4
Nigeria	89	6
Switzerland	81	5
Brazil	76	13
Denmark	73	8

FIJI

89% happy

- With 77% happy, Africa is the happiest region, followed by Latin America (74%) and Western Europe (59%). The unhappiest region is the Arab World with 27% saying they are unhappy.

- Males and females around the globe are level-pegging, with 53% of both sexes reporting they are happy. The happiest age group is the under 30s of which 57% say they are happy.

ROMANIA

THE 5 UNHAPPIEST

	HAPPY	UNHAPPY
Romania	28	39
Italy	35	10
Egypt	36	36
Russia	39	8
China	41	17

39% unhappy

ROAD FATALITIES

DEATHS ON THE ROADS, 2009

▸ 90% of all road traffic accidents worldwide occur in countries in the developing world where road safety is poor. India has the highest number of recorded road deaths with 105,725 in 2009.

Japan
5,772

South Korea
5,838

USA
33,808

▶ Road traffic accidents kill more people worldwide than malaria and are the leading cause of death for people aged 5–29 worldwide. Globally, every day c.3,500 people are killed in road traffic accidents.

▶ Road fatalities decreased in 2009, with the USA reaching their lowest fatality record for 50 years. Fatalities from motorcycles, however, increased in 13 of 29 countries since 2000.

Poland
4,752

Malaysia
6,745

Argentina
7,364

BROADBAND

% HOUSEHOLDS WITH
BROADBAND, 2011

▶ Regionally, the most broadband
subscribers are in South and East
Asia with a 28.9% share, followed
by western Europe with 22.5% and
North America with 18.4%. The
most popular method for receiving
broadband is via DSL (63.2%).

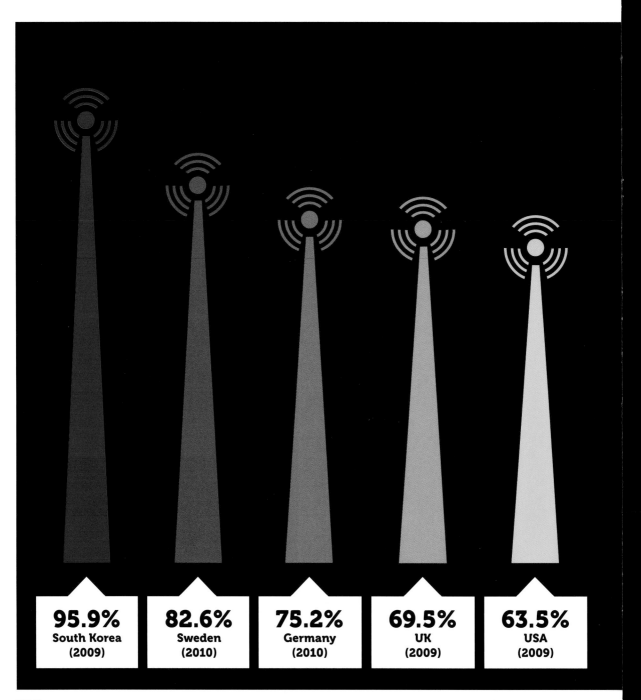

95.9%
South Korea
(2009)

82.6%
Sweden
(2010)

75.2%
Germany
(2010)

69.5%
UK
(2009)

63.5%
USA
(2009)

▶ In 2011, China had the most broadband subscribers in the world with 135.2 million, the USA was second with 88.7 million and Japan third with 34.6 million. By 2015 some 350 million new broadband customers will have be online.

▶ Growth in broadband subscriptions in 2011 was highest in South and East Asia with 7.6 million new customers. Wireless broadband is growing at a much faster rate than fixed wire broadband (14% as opposed to 2.3%).

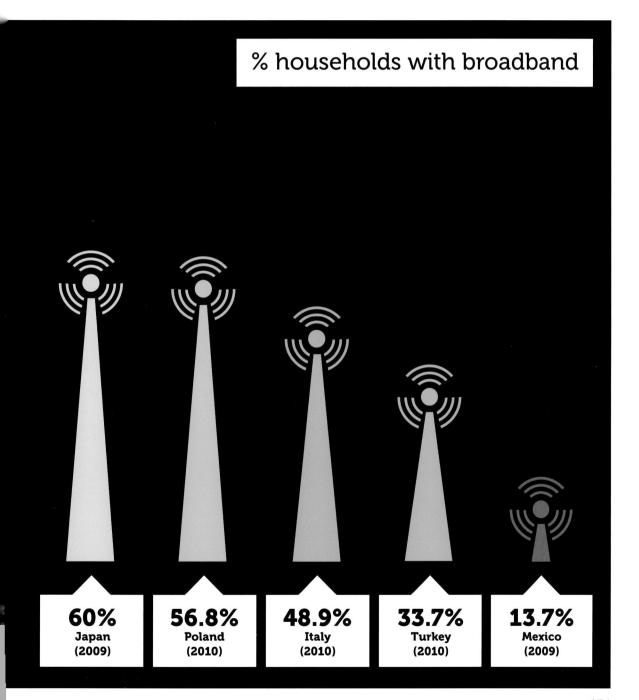

% households with broadband

60%	56.8%	48.9%	33.7%	13.7%
Japan (2009)	Poland (2010)	Italy (2010)	Turkey (2010)	Mexico (2009)

EDUCATION

% OF GDP SPENT ANNUALLY

▶ Free universal primary schooling is one of the United Nations Millennium Development Goals it hoped would be reached by 2015. However, there are currently 101 million children with no access to schooling, according to UNICEF.

DENMARK 7.8%

UK 5.5%

SOUTH KOREA 4.2%

POLAND 4.9%

ITALY 4.3%

KENYA 7%

FRANCE 5.6%

SPAIN 4.3%

GERMANY 4.5%

JAPAN 3.5%

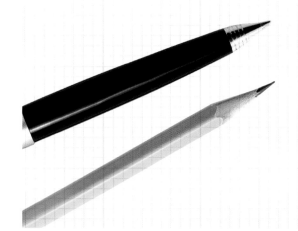

- In 2010 President Hamid Karzai of Afghanistan revealed that despite improvements some 42% of children in Afghanistan do not go to school. The world average spending on education is 4.4% of Gross Domestic Product.

- A 2010 study stated that improving overall educational standards affects a nation's GDP. If the USA closed the education gap between it and high achieving countries such as South Korea then it could add 16% to its GDP.

INDIA 3.1%   RUSSIA 3.9%

SWEDEN 6.6%

CUBA 13.6%

EQUATORIAL GUINEA 0.6%

USA 5.5%   AUSTRALIA 4.5%

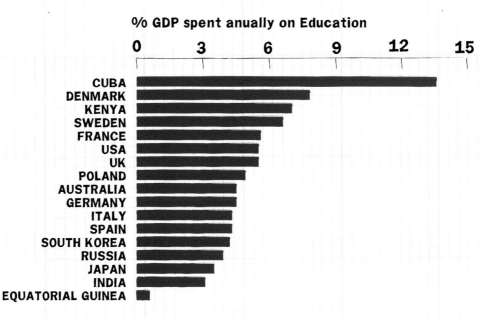

% GDP spent anually on Education

| 0 | 3 | 6 | 9 | 12 | 15 |

CUBA
DENMARK
KENYA
SWEDEN
FRANCE
USA
UK
POLAND
AUSTRALIA
GERMANY
ITALY
SPAIN
SOUTH KOREA
RUSSIA
JAPAN
INDIA
EQUATORIAL GUINEA

There are currently 23,574 nuclear weapons worldwide

down from a high of roughly 70,000 in the mid-1980s.

FIREARMS

% OF HOMICIDES WITH A FIREARM

▶ The percentage of homicides carried out with a firearm gives a good indication of the prevalence of guns in any one country. Gun ownership statistics are generally hard to come by as many firearms are not legally owned.

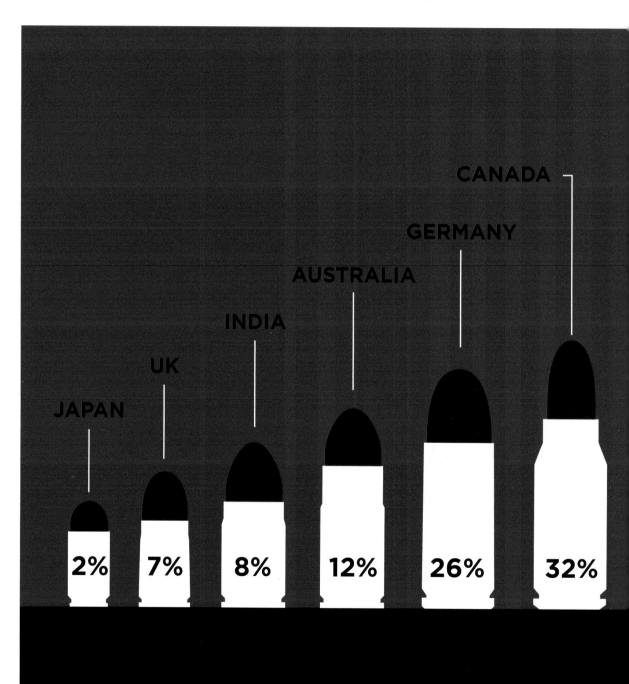

JAPAN — 2%

UK — 7%

INDIA — 8%

AUSTRALIA — 12%

GERMANY — 26%

CANADA — 32%

▶ It is estimated that there are 875 million small arms worldwide, which is enough for one gun for every ten people on earth. The USA has the biggest ratio of guns to people with 8.9 firearms for every ten people.

▶ In 2011 the Brazilian government announced a programme to reduce the number of guns in circulation before the 2014 World Cup. Brazilians will be given free tickets to the World Cup in return for any gun handed in to authorities.

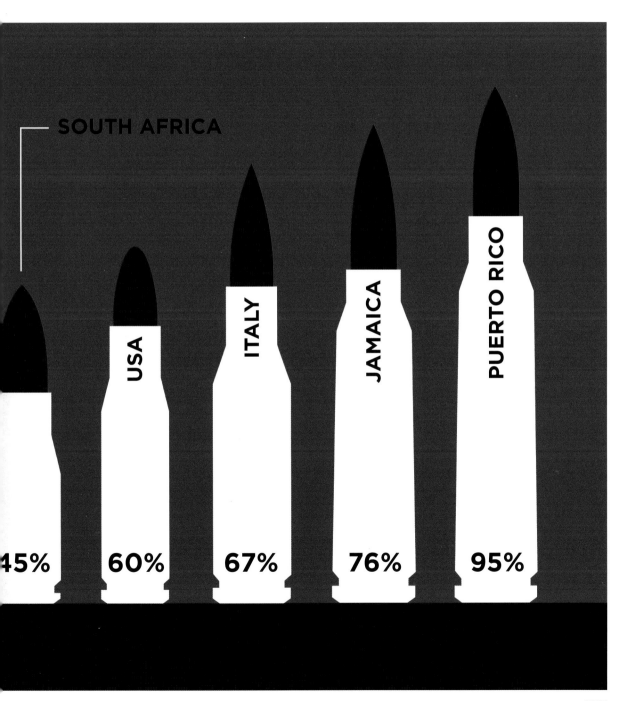

SOUTH AFRICA

USA

ITALY

JAMAICA

PUERTO RICO

45% 60% 67% 76% 95%

MARRIAGE

AVERAGE AGE AT MARRIAGE, 2008

▶ Worldwide, people have been getting married later in life. This has resulted in couples having their children later in life as well. Sweden has one of lowest marriage rates and, if trends persist, only 60% of all Swedish women will marry.

Sweden 34.3

Germany 33.7

France 33.4

Italy 33.3

Denmark 32.7

Ireland 32.4

South Korea 32

Australia 31.6

Spain 31.6

Japan 31.1

Canada 28.6

UK 28.1

Poland 28

USA 27.8

Saudi Arabia 27.2

New Zealand 27

Iran 26.4

Russia 26.3

Brazil 26.2

China 25.1

Nepal 22.4

The world's most expensive wedding was between the steel tycoon Lakshmi Mittal's daughter Vanisha and Amit Bhatia in 2004. The lavish celebration was reported to have cost in total approximately $78m.

In May 2011 Malta became the final country in the EU to legalize divorce. A 2009 survey stated that four kisses a day, a two-year-age gap and two romantic meals a month create a happy and long-lasting marriage.

Sweden 32.2
France 31.6
Ireland 31.4
Germany 31
Denmark 30.8
Italy 30
Australia 29.7
Japan 29.4
Spain 29.3
South Korea 28.8
Canada 26.6
UK 26.3
USA 26
New Zealand 25.6
Poland 25.3
Saudi Arabia 24.6
Russia 23.6
Iran 23.5
China 23.3
Brazil 23.1
Nepal 19.4

COCA-COLA

CONSUMPTION PER PERSON, 2011

▶ The blood orange flavoured Coca-Cola Light Sango is available only in Belgium, France and Luxembourg. Belgium consumes more Diet Coke per capita that any other country.

— MEXICO
— CHILE
— USA
— PANAMA
— ARGENTINA
— BELGIUM
— AUSTRALIA
— SPAIN
— CANADA
— AUSTRIA
— SOUTH AFRICA
— BOLIVIA
— BRAZIL
— UK
— PERU
— GERMANY
— EL SALVADOR
— JAPAN
— TURKEY
— FRANCE
— ITALY
— PHILIPPINES
— COLOMBIA
— THAILAND
— MOROCCO
— SOUTH KOREA
— RUSSIA
— EGYPT
— KENYA

BASED ON AN 8OZ SERVING

Includes, all drinks produced by the Coca-Cola Company, 78% of all Coca-Cola Company sales are of Coca-Cola not other brands.

▶ The only countries that sell Coke 2 are Yap in Micronesia and American Samoa. Introduced in 1985 as New Coke, it was replaced by classic Coke after a major consumer backlash.

▶ Latvia, Poland and Russia are the only countries in the world in which you can buy bottles of Coca-Cola Orange, a drink that was originally introduced into the UK and Gibraltar in 2007.

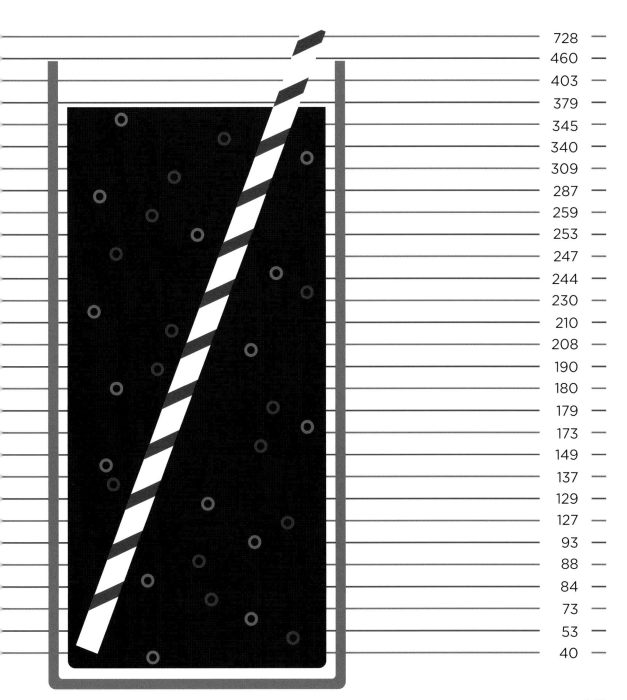

728
460
403
379
345
340
309
287
259
253
247
244
230
210
208
190
180
179
173
149
137
129
127
93
88
84
73
53
40

FRAUD

▶ According to the Global Economic Crime Survey, 2011, 34% of all respondents worldwide reported they had experienced economic crime in the previous 12 months.

% COMPANIES REPORTING FRAUD ANNUALLY, 2011

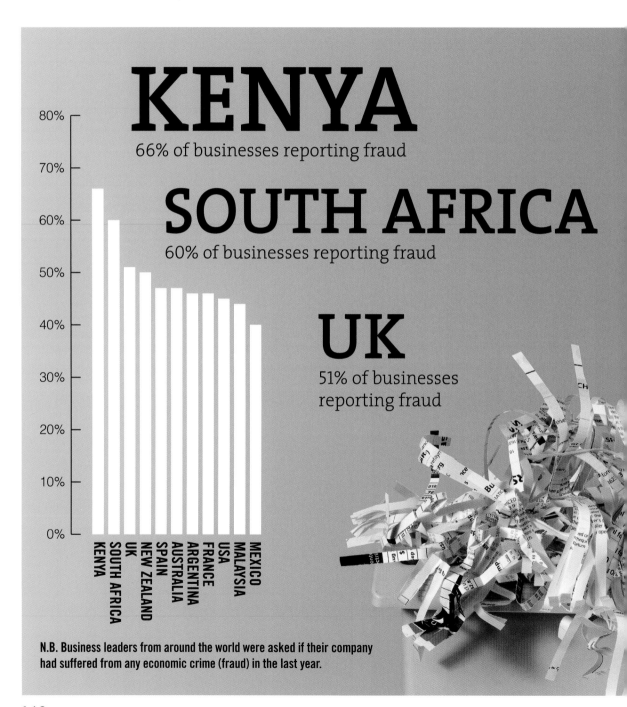

KENYA
66% of businesses reporting fraud

SOUTH AFRICA
60% of businesses reporting fraud

UK
51% of businesses reporting fraud

80%
70%
60%
50%
40%
30%
20%
10%
0%

KENYA
SOUTH AFRICA
UK
NEW ZEALAND
SPAIN
AUSTRALIA
ARGENTINA
FRANCE
USA
MALAYSIA
MEXICO

N.B. Business leaders from around the world were asked if their company had suffered from any economic crime (fraud) in the last year.

- 56% of those questioned revealed that the worst crimes committed had been an 'inside job', with nearly one in ten reporting losses of $5 million or more.

- The top four economic crimes reported were: asset misappropriation – 72%; accounting fraud – 24%; bribery and corruption – 24%; and cybercrime – 23%.

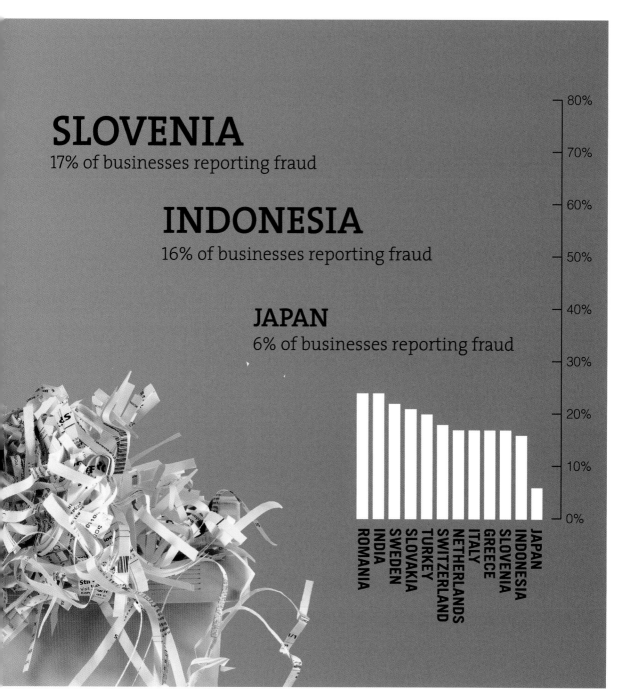

SLOVENIA
17% of businesses reporting fraud

INDONESIA
16% of businesses reporting fraud

JAPAN
6% of businesses reporting fraud

ROMANIA
INDIA
SWEDEN
SLOVAKIA
TURKEY
SWITZERLAND
NETHERLANDS
ITALY
GREECE
SLOVENIA
INDONESIA
JAPAN

80%
70%
60%
50%
40%
30%
20%
10%
0%

LANGUAGES

LANGUAGES WITH MOST SPEAKERS WORLDWIDE, 2009

▶ There are roughly 6,000 different spoken languages in the world. Of these, approximately 130 are endangered, which means they are spoken by ten or fewer people.

ENGLISH
328 MILLION

hello

RUSSIAN
144 MILLION

ПриБет

GERMAN
90 MILLION

hallo

PORTUGUESE
178 MILLION

olá

SPANISH
329 MILLION

hola

ARABIC
221 MILLION

مرحبا

- Mandarin is expected to grow in popularity as China's global trade increases. Aside from 645 million native speakers, 200 million speak Mandarin as a second language.

- Spanish is spoken in over 25 countries and is one of the official languages of the United Nations. The others are: Arabic, Chinese, English, French and Russian.

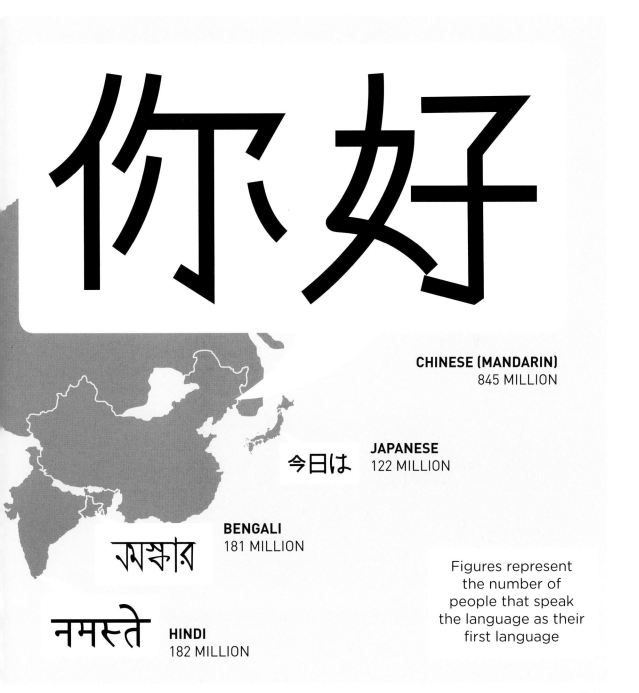

你好

CHINESE (MANDARIN)
845 MILLION

今日は **JAPANESE**
122 MILLION

BENGALI
181 MILLION
নমস্কার

নমস্তে **HINDI**
182 MILLION

Figures represent the number of people that speak the language as their first language

INTERNET

HOURS SPENT ONLINE PER
PERSON PER MONTH, 2010

▶ If you look at the number of
internet users per 100 inhabitants
(or internet penetration) then
Europe leads the way with 65%
of all Europeans online in 2010,
compared to 55% of Americans
and 30% across the whole world.

Hours spent online per month

CANADA	43.5
USA	35.3
UK	32.3
SOUTH KOREA	27.7
FRANCE	26.6
BRAZIL	25.8
GERMANY	24.1
RUSSIA	21.8
JAPAN	18.4
CHINA	13.5

0

▶ In 2010 there were more than 2 billion internet users, however, 65% of the world is not online at all. The average global internet user spends 14 hours a week online, the same amount of time most people spend watching TV every week.

▶ The price of receiving fixed-broadband dropped 18% in 2010. South Korea has the fastest internet speeds in the world with over 90% of internet users able to access the internet at speeds of over 10 Mbit/s.

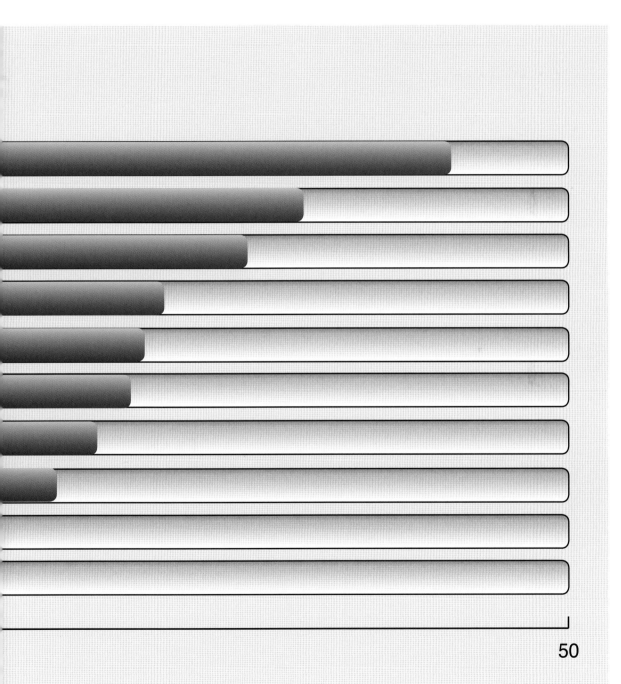

50

827 MILLION PEOPLE WORLDWIDE CURRENTLY LIVE IN A SLUM

– AN INCREASE OF 55 MILLION PEOPLE SINCE THE YEAR 2000.

HEALTH

HEALTH SPENDING AS % OF
GDP, 2007

▶ In 2008 the World Health
Organization reported that
healthcare is weighted towards
the rich. The wealthiest, who have
the least need, consume the most
care. The poorest with greater
need, tend to consume the least.

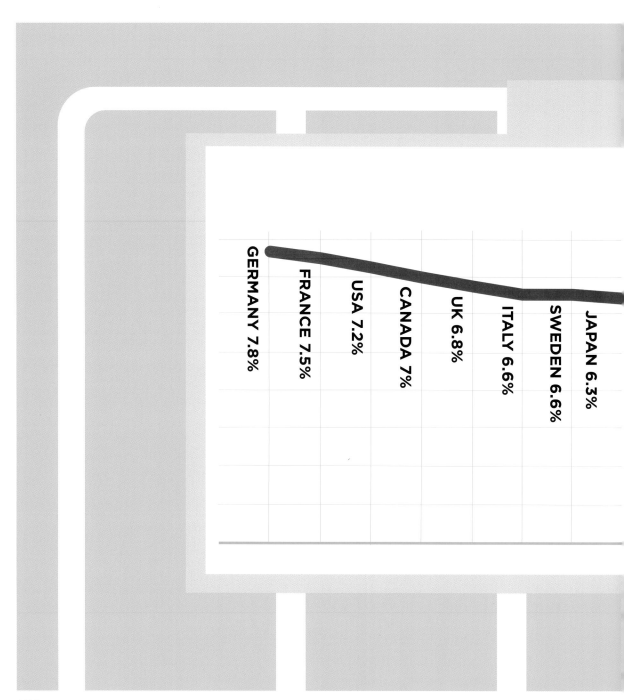

GERMANY 7.8%

FRANCE 7.5%

USA 7.2%

CANADA 7%

UK 6.8%

ITALY 6.6%

SWEDEN 6.6%

JAPAN 6.3%

▶ 100 million people every year fall into poverty worldwide because they are forced to pay for healthcare. France has the best healthcare in the world, according to a ranking created in 2000 by the World Health Organization.

▶ Austria has the highest density of doctors in the world with 4.8 physicians for every 1,000 people; compared with Japan that has the greatest number of hospital beds per capita, with 13.7 per 1,000 people in 2009.

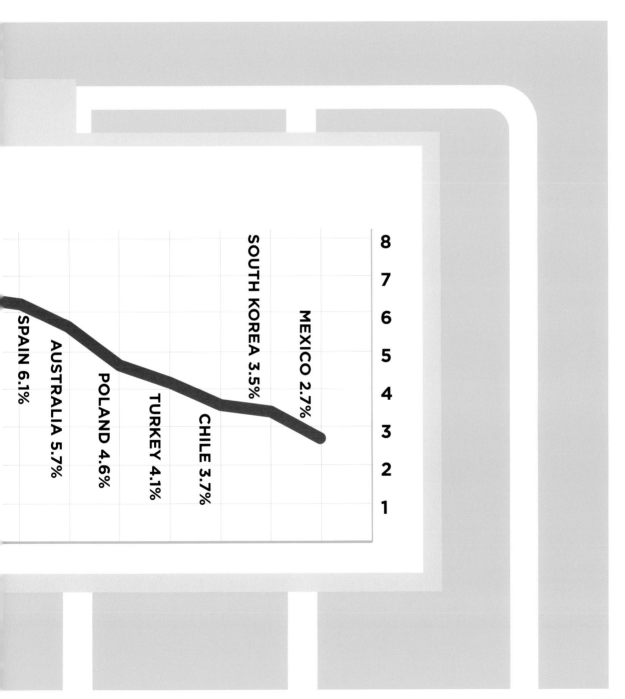

SPAIN 6.1%

AUSTRALIA 5.7%

POLAND 4.6%

TURKEY 4.1%

CHILE 3.7%

SOUTH KOREA 3.5%

MEXICO 2.7%

8 7 6 5 4 3 2 1

AID

TOP OVERSEAS AID
DONORS, 2010

▶ The United Nations (UN)
recommends that each country
donate 0.7% of their Gross National
Income (GNI) to development aid
but only a few countries do this,
they are: Denmark, Luxembourg,
Netherlands, Norway and Sweden.

Overseas Development Aid US $ millions 2010

Country: USA
30,154

Country: UK
13,763

Country: France
12,915

Country: Germany
12,723

Country: Japan
11,045

- Levels of Overseas Development Aid reached a record of $128.7bn in 2010. Although the USA is the greatest donor by amount, if you look at their donation in terms of a percentage of their Gross National Income (GNI) it only reaches 0.21%.

- The European Union (EU) has made it a target that all of the EU members of the Development Aid Committee (DAC) should be donating 0.7% of their Gross National Income (GNI) to aid by 2015.

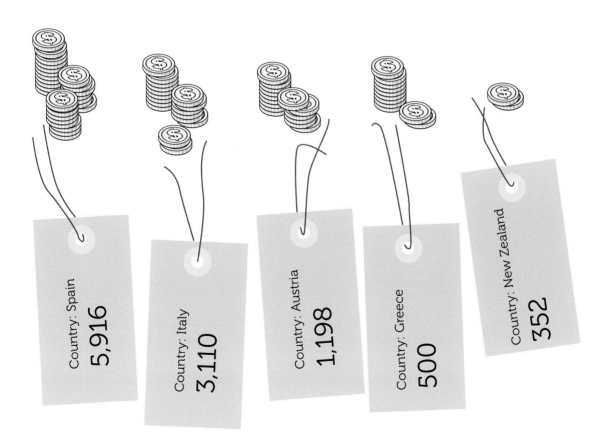

Country: Spain
5,916

Country: Italy
3,110

Country: Austria
1,198

Country: Greece
500

Country: New Zealand
352

UNEMPLOYMENT

% LABOUR FORCE WITHOUT A JOB, 2011

▶ 30 million jobs have been lost since the global economic crisis began in 2008. Youth unemployment is one of the greatest problems. The UN estimated that in 2009, 81 million young people aged 15–24 were out of work worldwide.

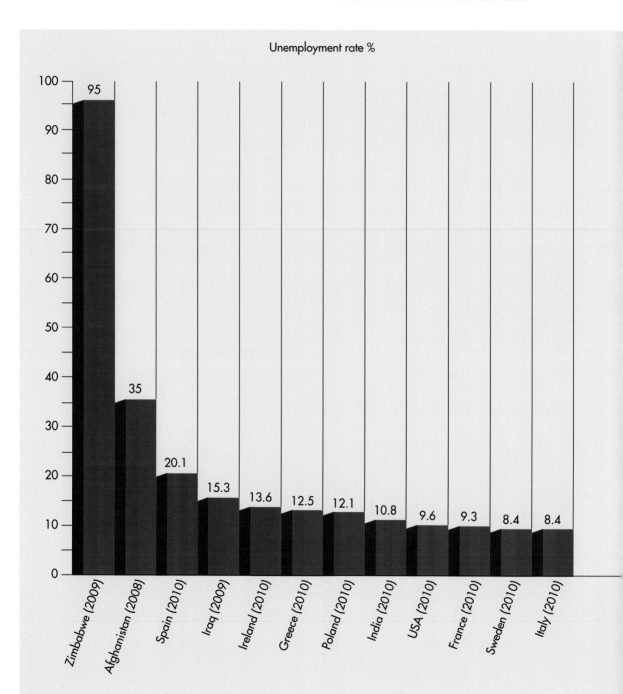

Unemployment rate %

Country (year)	Rate
Zimbabwe (2009)	95
Afghanistan (2008)	35
Spain (2010)	20.1
Iraq (2009)	15.3
Ireland (2010)	13.6
Greece (2010)	12.5
Poland (2010)	12.1
India (2010)	10.8
USA (2010)	9.6
France (2010)	9.3
Sweden (2010)	8.4
Italy (2010)	8.4

▶ Zimbabwe has the worst unemployment rate in the world with only 5% of the population in formal employment. In the last five years its economy has shrunk by 45% – many people now rely on the black market or charity to survive.

▶ A 2011 report suggested that 69 out of 118 countries surveyed had seen an increase in the percentage of people reporting that their living standard in 2010 had worsened in comparison to 2006.

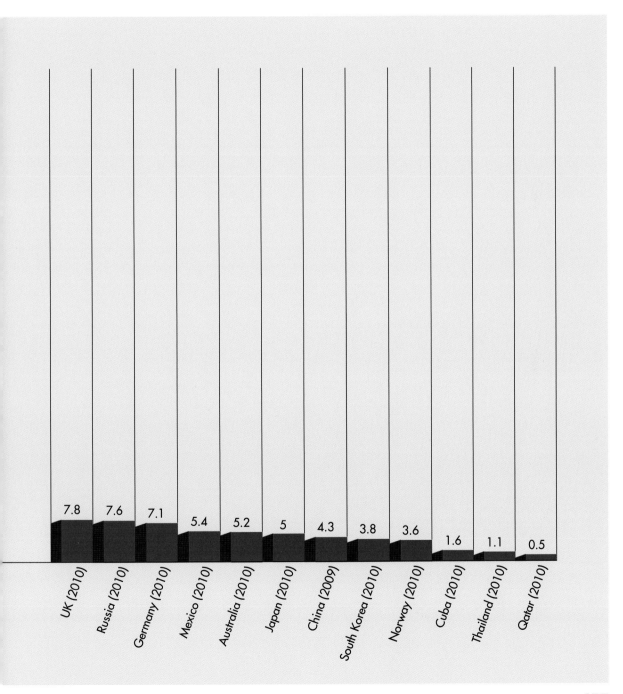

INFLATION

CONSUMER PRICES INFLATION, 2010

▶ In 2011, rising costs of food and gas saw an increase in inflation in most countries. Some believe this trend indicates that the global economy is rallying after several years of stagnation.

ZIMBABWE
24,411%

N.B. Consumer price index inflation relates to the annual percentage change in the cost for an average consumer to purchase a basket of goods.

▶ The debt crisis in Europe means the economy has been slow to recover. In contrast, China's economy has been growing so rapidly that its central bank has intervened to control rising prices.

▶ 1920s Germany suffered extreme hyperinflation when the economy was destroyed post-world war. Famously, wheelbarrows were loaded with bills to pay for a single loaf of bread.

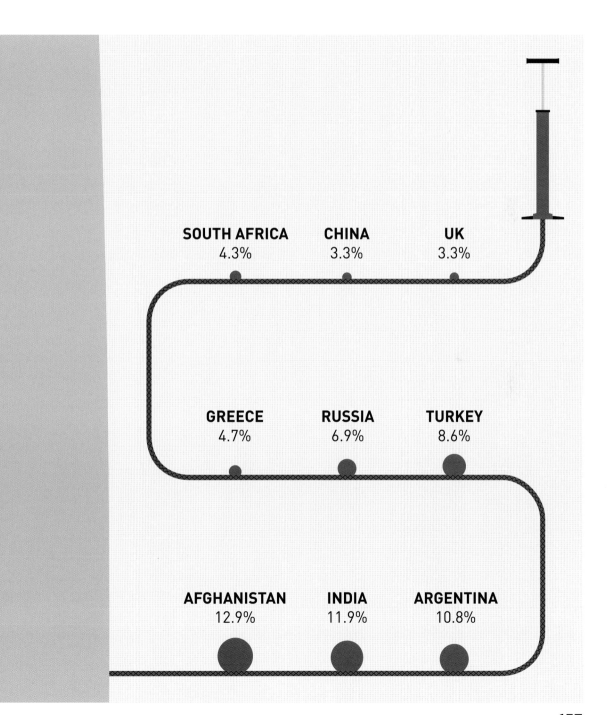

SOUTH AFRICA
4.3%

CHINA
3.3%

UK
3.3%

GREECE
4.7%

RUSSIA
6.9%

TURKEY
8.6%

AFGHANISTAN
12.9%

INDIA
11.9%

ARGENTINA
10.8%

SUICIDE

RATES PER 100,000, 2011

▶ Every year roughly one million people take their own lives; this equates to approximately 16 people in every 100,000. Males aged under 44 are the group most likely to commit suicide.

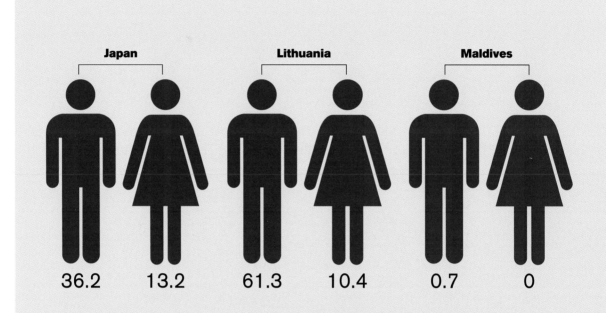

Japan
36.2   13.2

Lithuania
61.3   10.4

Maldives
0.7   0

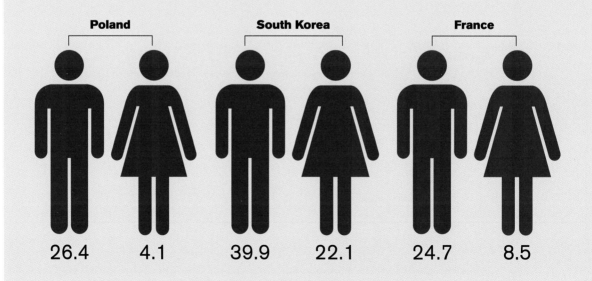

Poland
26.4   4.1

South Korea
39.9   22.1

France
24.7   8.5

▶ Suicide rates in the last 45 years have increased by 60%. Statistics tend not to record attempted suicides, which are up to twenty times more frequent than completed suicides.

▶ Globally, suicide is among the top twenty causes of death across all ages of the population. Regionally, Eastern Europe has by far the highest rate of suicide in the world.

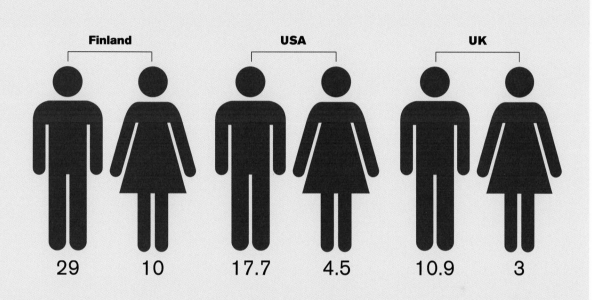

Finland
29   10

USA
17.7   4.5

UK
10.9   3

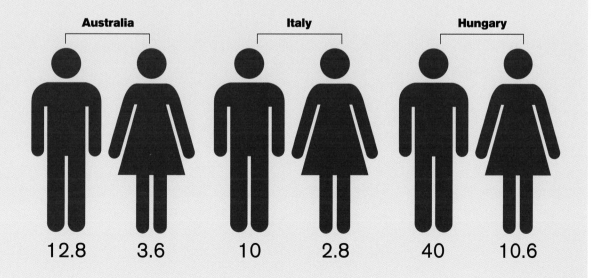

Australia
12.8   3.6

Italy
10   2.8

Hungary
40   10.6

UNDER 15s

% POPULATION UNDER 15, 2011

▶ The top ten countries in the world with the largest population of people under the age of 15 are all in Africa. According to the World Bank, 93% of Uganda's young people live on less than $2 a day.

EXERCISE 1, LIST THE COUNTRIES ON THE BLACKBOARD IN ORDER OF THE PERCENTAGE OF THE POPULATION WHO ARE UNDER 15 YEARS OF AGE (HIGHEST FIRST).

Country	% under 15
Niger	49
Uganda	48
Afghanistan	44
Iraq	43
Sudan	40
India	33
Mexico	29
Argentina	26
USA	20
Australia	19
France	18
Singapore	17
China	17

- In the developed world there are 4.1 adults of working age to support each child. However in the developing world where birth rates are higher the burden falls on just 1.3 working adults for each child.

- Around 90% of the world's 1.2 billion youth live in developing nations. Young people are moving away from rural areas into cities in search of work, leading to a swell in urban populations.

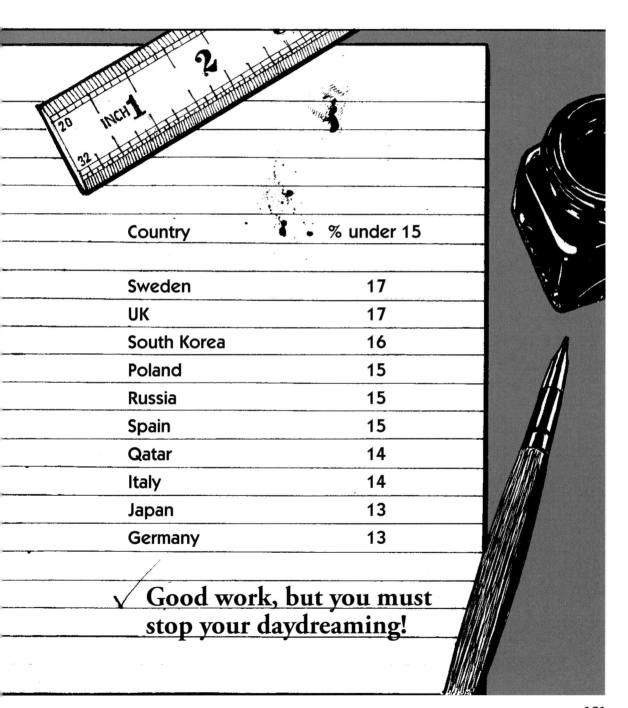

Country	% under 15
Sweden	17
UK	17
South Korea	16
Poland	15
Russia	15
Spain	15
Qatar	14
Italy	14
Japan	13
Germany	13

✓ **Good work, but you must stop your daydreaming!**

GLOBAL CARBON DIOXIDE

emissions reached
a peak of

394.97

parts per million in 2011
– the highest ever level.

According to readings taken from the US government's
Earth Systems Research Lab in Hawaii

In 1880 the carbon dioxide levels in the atmosphere were

285

parts per million.

TEENAGE SMOKING

% 15 AND UNDER WHO SMOKE CIGARETTES, 2010

▶ Teenagers who smoke are three times more likely to drink alcohol than non-smoking teenagers, eight times more likely to use marijuana and 22 times more likely to take cocaine.

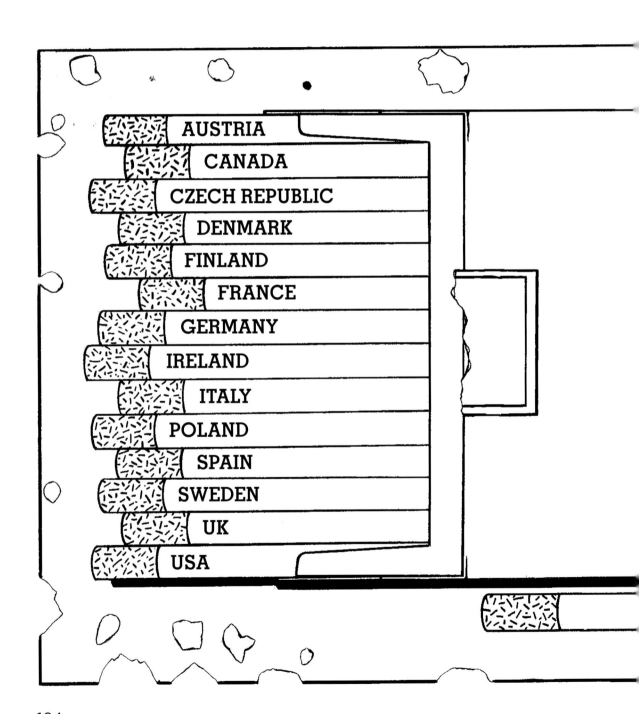

AUSTRIA
CANADA
CZECH REPUBLIC
DENMARK
FINLAND
FRANCE
GERMANY
IRELAND
ITALY
POLAND
SPAIN
SWEDEN
UK
USA

Across the developed world teenage smoking has dropped significantly, probably due to more stringent laws on smoking in public places and greater awareness of the health risks.

In general, 15-year-old girls are more likely to smoke than 15-year-old boys. Lebanon has the highest rate of teen smoking in the world, with 60% of teens smoking regularly.

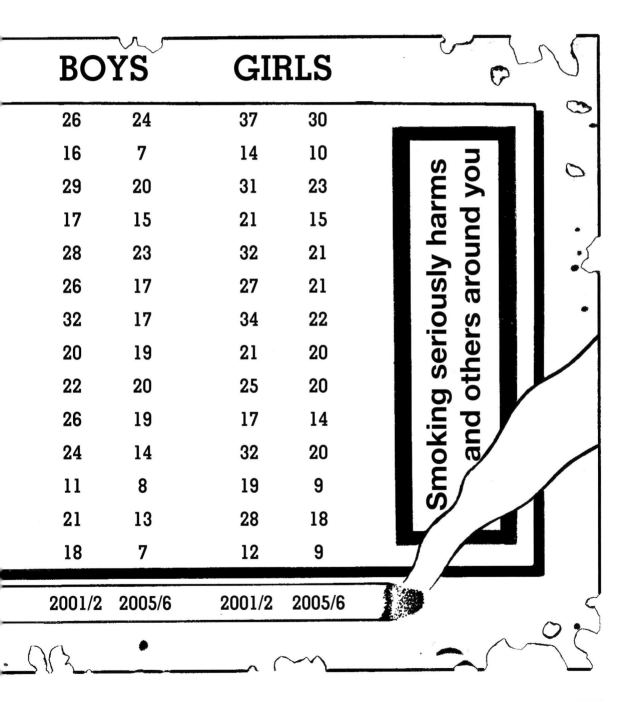

BOYS		GIRLS	
26	24	37	30
16	7	14	10
29	20	31	23
17	15	21	15
28	23	32	21
26	17	27	21
32	17	34	22
20	19	21	20
22	20	25	20
26	19	17	14
24	14	32	20
11	8	19	9
21	13	28	18
18	7	12	9
2001/2	2005/6	2001/2	2005/6

Smoking seriously harms and others around you

EXECUTIONS

NUMBER OF EXECUTIONS, 2010

▶ 58 countries allow the death penalty but less than half executed anyone in 2010. There were at least 17,833 people held worldwide under sentence of death. China executed more people than the rest of the world put together.

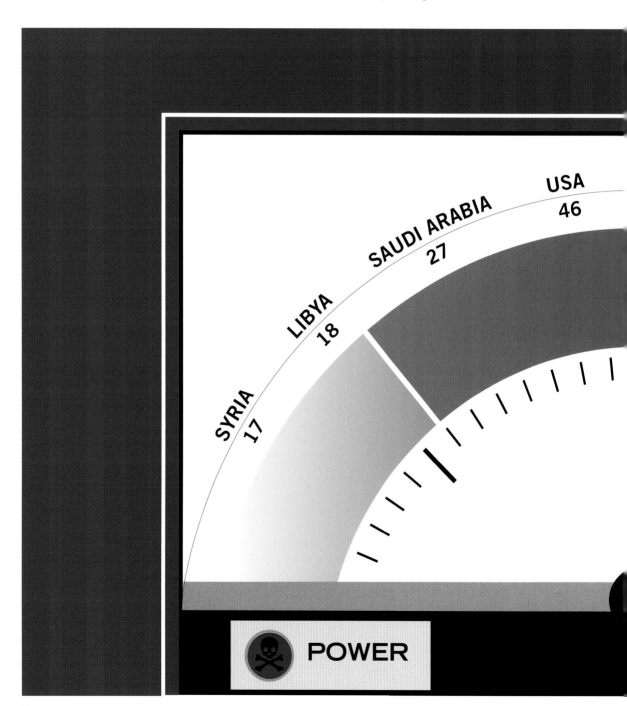

USA
46

SAUDI ARABIA
27

LIBYA
18

SYRIA
17

☠ POWER

▶ The trend for utilizing the death penalty is decreasing. 23 countries carried out executions in 2010, down from an average of 40 countries in the mid-1990s. 96 countries have abolished the death penalty for all crimes.

▶ Execution methods used in 2010 included: beheading (Saudi Arabia); eletrocution (USA); hanging (Bangladesh, Botswana, Egypt, Syria); lethal injection (China, USA); and shooting (Bahrain, Somalia, Vietnam, Yemen).

N.B. These figures should be treated as the minimum numbers executed. Due to government secrecy over the issue, many countries do not reveal official statistics.

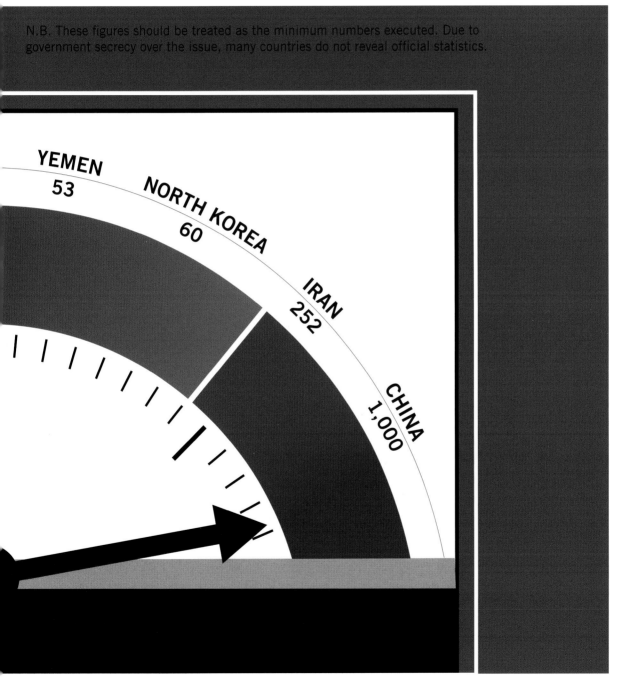

YEMEN
53

NORTH KOREA
60

IRAN
252

CHINA
1,000

CHESAREANS

PER 1,000 LIVE BIRTHS, 2008/9

▶ A 2010 report by the World Health Organization revealed that 46% of all the births reviewed in China were caesarean sections, at least a quarter of which were not medically required.

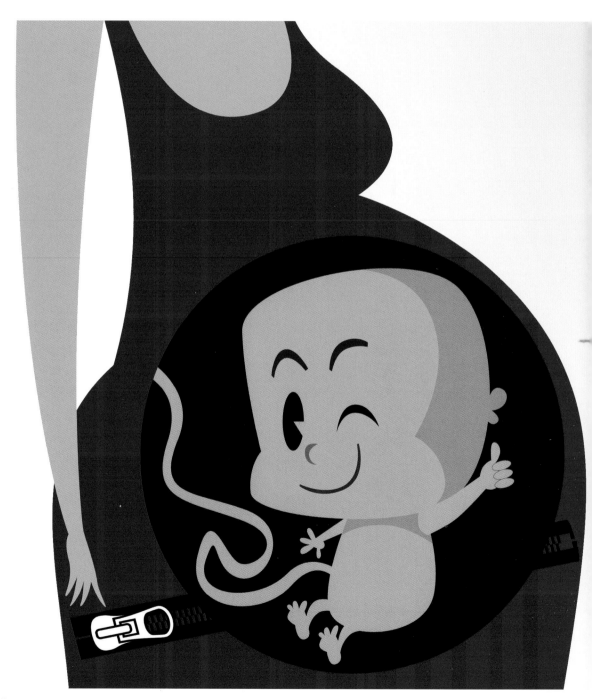

▶ The World Health Organization recommends that the caesarean rate should not be higher than 10–15% of all births. Unnecessary caesareans are more costly than natural births.

▶ Italy is the safest place to give birth, with four maternal deaths for every 100,000 live births. Afghanistan is the most dangerous, with 1,575 maternal deaths for every 100,000 live births.

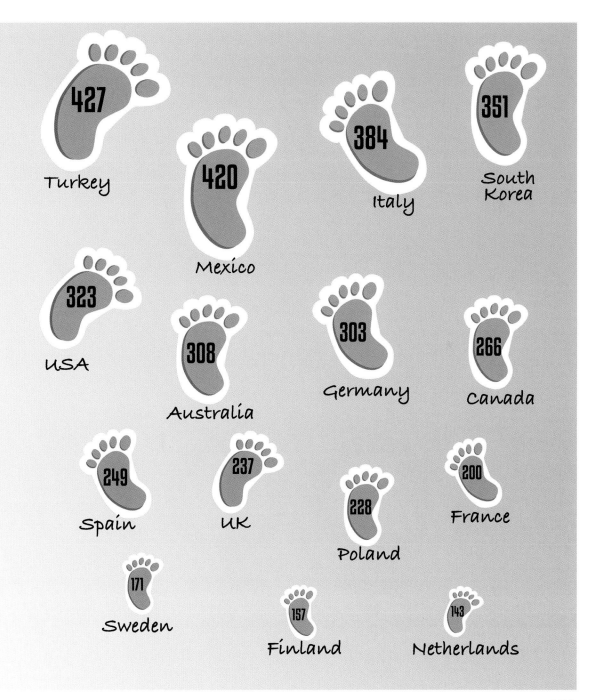

427 Turkey

420 Mexico

384 Italy

351 South Korea

323 USA

308 Australia

303 Germany

266 Canada

249 Spain

237 UK

228 Poland

200 France

171 Sweden

157 Finland

143 Netherlands

VIOLENCE

ATTITUDES TO VIOLENCE
AGAINST WOMEN, 2005

▶ A 2005 report revealed that
54% of Ethiopian women in
relationships reported at least
one instance of physical or sexual
violence from a partner in the
space of one year, compared
to 4% of women in Japan.

% agreeing that it is 'never
justifiable for a man to
beat his wife'

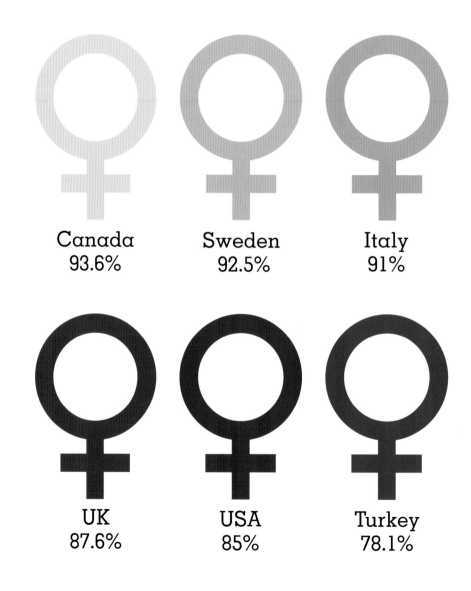

Canada
93.6%

Sweden
92.5%

Italy
91%

UK
87.6%

USA
85%

Turkey
78.1%

▶ Research that has been conducted in the USA suggests that boys who witness their fathers being violent are ten times more likely to go on to abuse a spouse than boys that are brought up in non-violent homes.

▶ Pakistan has an especially high rate of violence against women, with 8,000 incidents reported in 2010 according to the non-governmental organization Aurat Foundation. 557 of these reported incidents involved so-called honour killings.

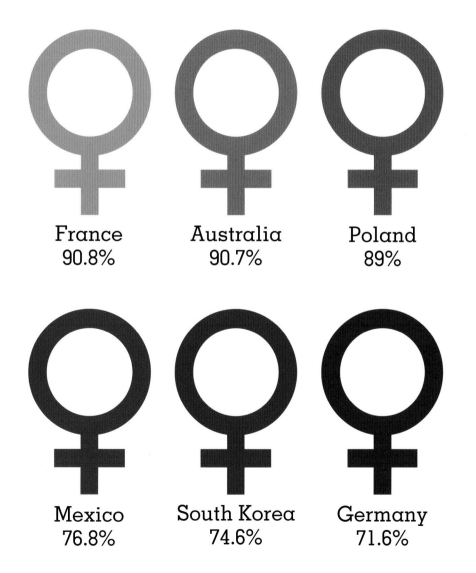

France
90.8%

Australia
90.7%

Poland
89%

Mexico
76.8%

South Korea
74.6%

Germany
71.6%

GDP

GROSS DOMESTIC PRODUCT (GDP) PER CAPITA, 2011

▶ GDP per capita is used as a marker of a nation's economy and therefore the expected standard of living. Regionally, Europe has the highest GDP per capita, and sub-Saharan Africa the lowest.

AUSTRALIA $42,131 US

DENMARK $55,998 US

GERMANY $40,509 US

IRELAND $45,497 US

JAPAN $43,137 US

LUXEMBOURG $108,921 US

NORWAY $84,840 US

SWEDEN $48,832 US

SWITZERLAND $66,934 US

USA $47,184 US

▶ Research in 2011 suggested that a one-year increase in the life expectancy of a population can add almost 4% to the GDP per capita. China has seen the largest growth in GDP in the last 4 years.

▶ According to *The Economist* magazine, since the recession began most wealthy countries have seen their GDP per capita drop. In Ireland and Greece it has dropped by 20 to 25%.

N.B. GDP per capita is a measure of all the goods and services produced by a country and divided by the number of residents. It is a good measure of a country's economic output and standard of living.

Roughly one third of all **food produced** for human consumption globally **is wasted** each year – that is **1.3 billion tonnes** of **food waste** each year.

FOREIGN-BORN POPULATION

AS % OF TOTAL POPULATION

▶ In Luxembourg in 2009, 57% of 15-year-olds had a least one foreign-born parent. In the UAE 71% of the total population is made up of immigrants.

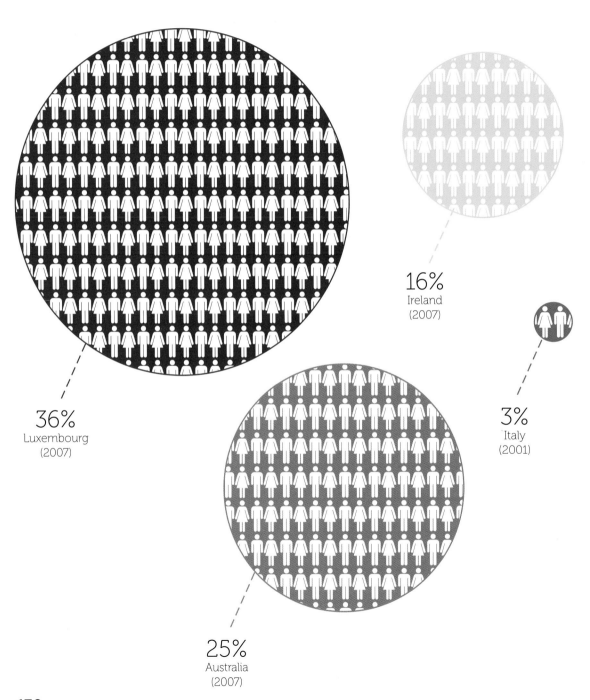

36%
Luxembourg
(2007)

16%
Ireland
(2007)

25%
Australia
(2007)

3%
Italy
(2001)

▶ Countries with a relatively low proportion of foreign-born residents, such as Mexico, Turkey and Poland, are generally among the less wealthy nations.

▶ There were 190,634,000 immigrants in 2006, that represents 3% of the world's population. 61% of immigrants have settled in the developed world.

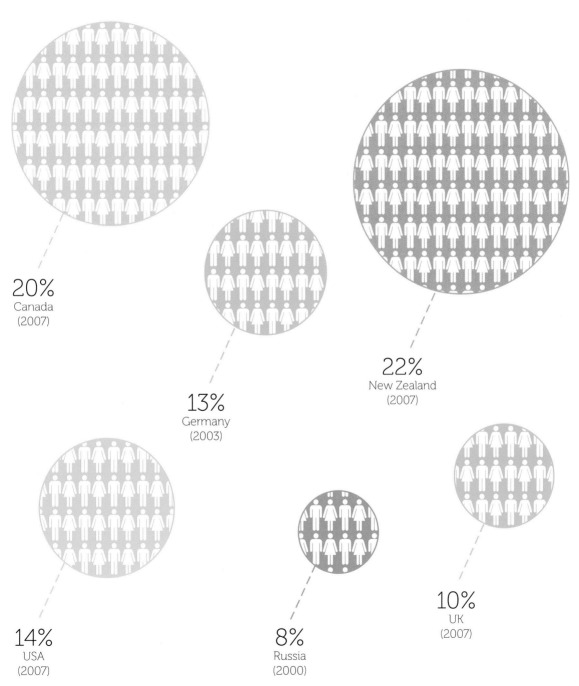

20%
Canada
(2007)

13%
Germany
(2003)

22%
New Zealand
(2007)

14%
USA
(2007)

8%
Russia
(2000)

10%
UK
(2007)

PRISONS

% POPULATION IN PRISON, 2009

▶ Over 9.8 million people are held in jails globally. A large proportion of this number is accounted for the USA, China and Russia. San Marino, (population 30,000) has just one prisoner.

HIGHEST PRISON POPULATION RATES (PER 100,000)

PRISON POPULATION RATE (PER 100,000)	
USA	756
Russia	629
S. Africa	335
Israel	326
Thailand	257
Brazil	227
Iran	222
Poland	221
Libya	209
Mexico	207

1. USA
756

2. RUSSIA
629

5. THAILAND
257

6. BRAZIL
227

- The world's largest jail in terms of size (not capacity) is the Twin Towers Correctional Facility in Los Angeles, California. The complex measures 140,000m² and was opened in 1997.

- The world median prison population rate is 125. The high numbers of people in USA jails can partially be explained by the relatively high levels of violent crime and the availability of guns.

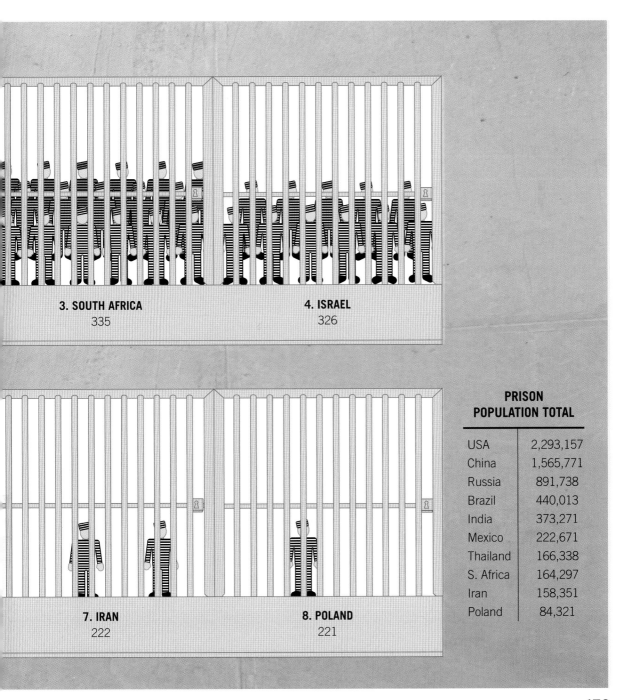

3. SOUTH AFRICA
335

4. ISRAEL
326

7. IRAN
222

8. POLAND
221

PRISON POPULATION TOTAL

USA	2,293,157
China	1,565,771
Russia	891,738
Brazil	440,013
India	373,271
Mexico	222,671
Thailand	166,338
S. Africa	164,297
Iran	158,351
Poland	84,321

ASSISTED SUICIDE

NUMBERS OF ASSISTED SUICIDES AT DIGNITAS, 1998-2009

▶ Assisted suicide is suicide brought about with the help of another person, particularly a doctor. It is lawful in Switzerland, Luxembourg, Belgium, the Netherlands and the states of Montana, Oregon and Washington in the USA.

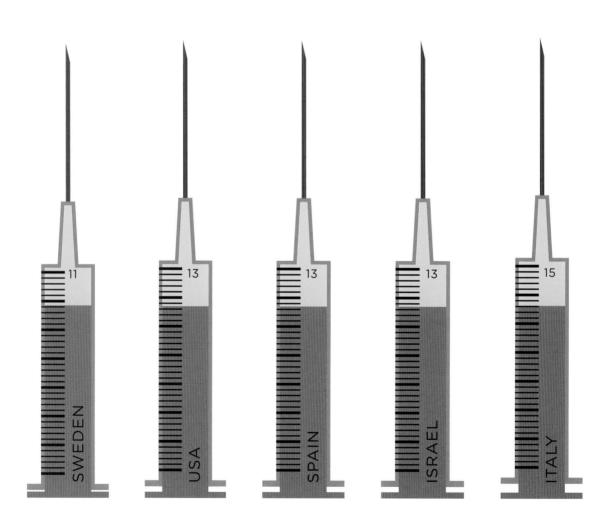

SWEDEN 11

USA 13

SPAIN 13

ISRAEL 13

ITALY 15

- Ireland, Italy and Canada all have laws that outlaw assisted suicide. The clinic Dignitas in Switzerland was founded by the lawyer, Ludwig Minelli and allows people to travel from around the world to its premises to commit suicide.

- Over 1,040 people with terminal illness or **severe** physical or mental illnesses have been helped to die at the Dignitas clinic since it was founded in 1998. They are not the only assisted suicide organization in Switzerland.

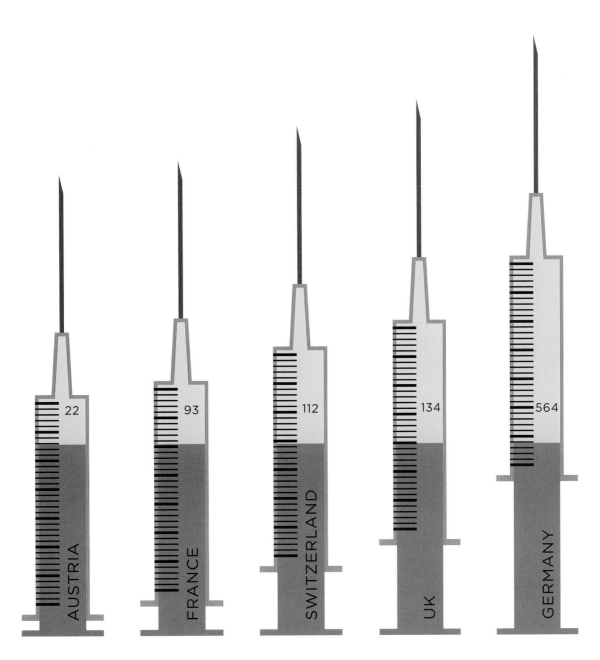

AUSTRIA 22

FRANCE 93

SWITZERLAND 112

UK 134

GERMANY 564

COUNTRIES BY SIZE
(SQUARE KILOMETRES)

Country Area	(square kilometres)		
Afghanistan	652,230	Canada	9,984,670
Albania	28,748	Cape Verde	4,033
Algeria	2,381,741	Cayman Islands	264
American Samoa	199	Central African Republic	622,984
Andorra	468	Chad	1,284,000
Angola	1,246,700	Chile	756,102
Anguilla	91	China	9,596,961
Antarctica	14,000,000	Christmas Island	135
Antigua and Barbuda	442.6	Colombia	1,138,910
Argentina	2,780,400	Comoros	2,235
Armenia	29,743	Cook Island	236
Aruba	180	Costa Rica	51,100
Australia	7,741,220	Cote d'Ivoire	322,463
Austria	83,871	Croatia	56,594
Azerbaijan	86,600	Cuba	110,860
		Curacao	444
Bahrain	760	Cyprus	9,251
Bangladesh	143,998	Czech Rep	78,867
Barbados	430		
Belarus	207,600	Denmark	43,094
Belgium	30,528	Djibouti	23,200
Belize	22,966	Dominica	751
Benin	112,622	Dominican Republic	48,670
Bermuda	54	DR Congo	2,344,858
Bhutan	38,394		
Bolivia	1,098,581	Ecuador	283,561
Bosnia and Herzegovina	51,197	Egypt	1,001,450
Botswana	581,730	El Salvador	21,041
Brazil	8,514,877	Equatorial Guinea	28,051
British Virgin Islands	151	Eritrea	117,600
Brunei	5,765	Estonia	45,228
Bulgaria	110,879	Ethiopia	1,104,300
Burkina Faso	274,200		
Burma	676,578	Falkland Islands	12,173
Burundi	27,830	Faroe Islands	1,393
		Fiji	18,274
Cambodia	181,035	Finland	338,145
Cameroon	475,440	France	551,500

French Polynesia	4,167	Latvia	64,589
		Lebanon	10,400
Gabon	267,667	Lesotho	30,355
Gaza Strip	360	Liberia	111,369
Georgia	69,700	Libya	1,759,540
Germany	357,022	Liechtenstein	160
Ghana	238,533	Lithuania	65,300
Gibraltar	6.5	Luxembourg	2,586
Greece	131,957		
Greenland	2,166,086	Macau	28.2
Grenada	344	Macedonia	25,713
Guam	544	Madagascar	587,041
Guatemala	108,889	Malawi	118,484
Guernsey	78	Malaysia	329,847
Guinea	245,857	Maldives	298
Guinea-Bissau	36,125	Mali	1,240,192
Guyana	214,969	Malta	316
		Marshall Islands	181
Haiti	27,750	Mauritania	1,030,700
Holy See (Vatican City)	0.44	Mauritius	2,040
Honduras	112,090	Mexico	1,964,375
Hong Kong	1,104	Micronesia,	702
Hungary	93,028	Federated States of	
		Moldova	33,851
Iceland	103,000	Monaco	2
India	3,287,263	Mongolia	1,564,116
Indonesia	1,904,569	Montenegro	13,812
Iran	1,648,195	Montserrat	102
Iraq	438,317	Morrocco	446,550
Ireland	70,273	Mozambique	799,380
Isle of Man	572		
Israel	20,770	Namibia	824,292
Italy	301,340	Nauru	21
		Nepal	147,181
Jamaica	10,991	Netherlands	41,543
Japan	377,915	New Caledonia	18,575
Jersey	116	New Zealand	267,710
Jordan	89,342	Nicaragua	130,370
		Niger	1,267,000
Kazakhstan	2,724,900	Nigeria	923,768
Kenya	580,367	Niue	260
Kiribati	811	Norfolk Island	36
Kosovo	10,887	North Korea	120,538
Kuwait	17,818	Northern Mariana Islands	464
Kyrgyzstan	199,951	Norway	323,802
Laos	236,800	Oman	309,500

Pakistan	796,095	Sudan	1,861,484
Palau	459	Suriname	163,820
Panama	75,420	Svalbard	62,045
Papua New Guinea	462,840	Swaziland	17,364
Paraguay	406,752	Sweden	450,295
Peru	1,285,216	Switzerland	41,277
Philippines	300,000	Syria	185,180
Pitcairn Islands	47		
Poland	312,685	Taiwan	35,980
Portugal	92,090	Tajikistan	143,100
Puerto Rico	13,790	Tanzania	947,300
		Thailand	513,120
Qatar	11,586	The Bahamas	13,880
		The Gambia	11,295
Republic of Congo	342,000	Timor-Leste	14,874
Romania	238,391	Togo	56,785
Russia	17,098,242	Tokelau	12
Rwanda	26,338	Tonga	747
		Trinidad and Tobago	5,128
Saint Barthelemy	21	Tunisia	163,610
Saint Helena, Ascension,	308	Turkey	783,562
and Tristan da Cunha		Turkmenistan	488,100
Saint Kitts and Nevis	261	Turks and Caicos Islands	948
Saint Lucia	616	Tuvalu	26
Saint Martin	54.4		
Saint Pierre and Miquelon	242	UAE	83,600
Saint Vincent and the	389	Uganda	241,038
Grenadines		UK	243,610
Samoa	2,831	Ukraine	603,550
San Marino	61	Uruguay	176,215
Sao Tome and Principe	964	USA	9,826,675
Saudi Arabia	2,149,690	Uzbekistan	447,400
Senegal	196,722		
Serbia	77,474	Vanuatu	12,189
Seychelles	455	Venezuela	912,050
Sierra Leone	71,740	Vietnam	331,210
Singapore	697	Virgin Islands	1,910
Sint Maarten	34		
Slovakia	49,035	Wallis and Futuna	142
Slovenia	20,273	West Bank	5,860
Solomon Islands	28,896	Western Sahara	266,000
Somalia	637,657		
South Africa	1,219,090	Yemen	527,968
South Korea	99,720		
South Sudan	644,329	Zambia	752,618
Spain	505,370	Zimbabwe	390,757
Sri Lanka	65,610		

COUNTRIES BY POPULATION
(MILLIONS)

Country	population (millions)		Country	population (millions)
China	1.3bn		Iraq	31.1
India	1.2bn		Afghanistan	30.4
USA	313.8		Nepal	29.9
Indonesia	248.2		Peru	29.5
Brazil	205.7		Malaysia	29.2
Pakistan	190.3		Uzbekistan	28.4
Nigeria	170.1		Venezuela	28
Bangladesh	161.1		Saudi Arabia	26.5
Russia	138.1		Ghana	25.2
Japan	127.4		Yemen	24.8
Mexico	115		North Korea	24.6
Philippines	103.8		Mozambique	23.5
Ethiopia	93.8		Taiwan	23.1
Vietnam	91.5		Madagascar	22.6
Egypt	83.7		Syria	22.5
Germany	81.3		Australia	22
Turkey	79.7		Cote d'Ivoire	22
Iran	78.9		Romania	21.8
DR Congo	73.6		Sri Lanka	21.5
Thailand	67.1		Cameroon	20.1
UK	63		Angola	18.1
France	62.8		Kazakhstan	17.5
Italy	61.3		Burkina Faso	17.3
Burma	54.6		Chile	17.1
South Korea	48.9		Niger	17.1
South Africa	48.8		Netherlands	16.7
Spain	47		Malawi	16.3
Colombia	45.2		Ecuador	15.2
Ukraine	44.9		Cambodia	15
Tanzania	43.6		Mali	14.5
Kenya	43		Zamba	14.3
Argentina	42.2		Guatemala	14.1
Poland	38.4		Senegal	12.9
Uganda	35.9		Zimbabwe	12.6
Algeria	35.4		Rwanda	11.7
Canada	34.3		Cuba	11.1
Sudan	34.2		Chad	11
Morocco	32.3		Guinea	10.9

Greece	10.8	Croatia	4.5
Portugal	10.8	Republic of Congo	4.4
Tunisia	10.7	New Zealand	4.3
Burundi	10.6	Lebanon	4.1
South Sudan	10.6	Puerto Rico	4
Belgium	10.4	Liberia	3.9
Bolivia	10.3	Moldova	3.7
Czech Rep	10.2	Lithuania	3.5
Dominican Republic	10.1	Panama	3.5
Somalia	10.1	Mauritania	3.4
Hungary	10	Uruguay	3.3
Haiti	9.8	Mongolia	3.2
Benin	9.6	Oman	3.1
Azerbaijan	9.5	Albania	3
Belarus	9.5	Armenia	3
Sweden	9.1	Jamaica	2.9
Honduras	8.3	Kuwait	2.6
Austria	8.2	West Bank	2.6
Tajikistan	7.8	Latvia	2.2
Switzerland	7.7	Namibia	2.2
Israel	7.6	Botswana	2.1
Serbia	7.3	Macedonia	2.1
Hong Kong	7.2	Slovenia	2
Bulgaria	7	Lesotho	1.9
Togo	7	Qatar	1.9
Libya	6.7	The Gambia	1.8
Laos	6.6	Kosovo	1.8
Jordan	6.5	Gaza Strip	1.7
Paraguay	6.5	Gabon	1.6
Papua New Guinea	6.3	Guinea-Bissau	1.6
El Salvador	6.1	Swaziland	1.4
Eritrea	6.1	Estonia	1.3
Nicaragua	5.7	Mauritius	1.3
Denmark	5.5	Bahrain	1.2
Kyrgyzstan	5.5	Timor-Leste	1.2
Sierra Leone	5.5	Trinidad and Tobago	1.2
Slovakia	5.5	Cyprus	1.1
Singapore	5.4		
Finland	5.3		
UAE	5.3		
Turkmenistan	5.1		
Central African Republic	5		
Norway	4.7		
Ireland	4.7		
Bosnia and Herzegovina	4.6		
Costa Rica	4.6		
Georgia	4.6		

Countries <1m	Thousands
Fiji	890,057
Djibouti	774,389
Guyana	741,908
Comoros	737,284
Bhutan	716,896
Equatorial Guinea	685,991
Montenegro	657,394
Solomon Islands	584,578
Macau	578,025
Suriname	560,157
Cape Verde	523568
Western Sahara	522,928
Luxembourg	509,074
Malta	409,836
Brunei	408,786
Maldives	394,451
Belize	327,719
The Bahamas	316,182
Iceland	313,183
Barbados	287,733
French Polynesia	274,512
New Caledonia	260,166
Vanuatu	227,574
Samoa	194,320
Guam	185,674
Sao Tome and Principe	183,176
Saint Lucia	162,178
Curacao	142,180
Virgin Islands	109,574
Grenada	109,011
Aruba	107,635
Micronesia, Federated States of	106,487
Tonga	106,146
Saint Vincent and the Grenadines	103,537
Kiribati	101,998
Jersey	94,949
Seychelles	90,024
Antigua and Barbuda	89,018
Isle of Man	85,421
Andorra	85,082
Dominica	73,126
Bermuda	69,080
Marshall Islands	68,480

American Samoa	68,061
Guernsey	65,345
Greenland	57,695
Cayman Islands	52,560
Saint Kitts and Nevis	50,726
Faroe Islands	49,483
Turks and Caicos Islands	46,335
Northern Mariana Islands	44,582
Sint Maarten	37,429
Liechtenstein	36,713
San Marino	32,140
British Virgin Islands	31,148
Saint Martin	30,959
Monaco	30,510
Gibraltar	29,034
Palau	21,032
Wallis and Futuna	15,453
Anguilla	15,423
Cook Island	10,777
Tuvalu	10,619
Nauru	9,378
Saint Helena, Ascension, and Tristan da Cunha	7,728
Saint Barthelemy	7,332
Saint Pierre and Miquelon	5,831
Montserrat	5,164
Falkland Islands	3,140
Norfolk Island	2,182
Svalbard	1,970
Christmas Island	1,496
Tokelau	1,368
Niue	1,269
Holy See (Vatican City)	836
Pitcairn Islands	48

SOURCES

Literacy
- Central Intelligence Agency World Factbook, 2011 – Literacy
- The World Bank – Data – Education – Literacy rate, adult total (% of people ages 15 and above)
- United Nations Millenium Development Goals
- Africa Renewal, Abolishing fees boosts African schooling [Online]

Computers
- Pew Global Attitudes Project, *World Publics Welcome Global Trade – But Not Immigration* [Online]
- iSuppli, *Lenovo Jumps to No. 2 PC Rank in Q3, Challenging HP's Lead* [Online]

Gambling Losses
- CNBC, *World's Biggest Gambling Nations* [Online]
- Australian National University, *Public Opinion on Gambling*, July 2011

Drunkenness
- Health Behaviour in School-Aged Children (HBSC), 2009
- Health Behaviour in School-Aged Children (HBSC), *Social determinants of health and well-being among young people*

Hours Worked
- OECD Employment and Labour Markets – Average Annual Working Time 2010
- Forbes, *The World's Hardest Working Countries* [Online]
- Forbes, *Why Europeans Work Less Than Americans* [Online]
- CNBC, *The World's Hardest Working Nations* [Online]

Cars
- The World Bank – Data – Infrastructure – Passenger Cars (per 1000 people)
- PricewaterhouseCoopers, *Autofacts Global Automotive Outlook, 2008 Q2 Release* [Online]
- MSN Cars
- Forbes, *The World's Most Popular Cars* [Online]

Heritage Sites
- UNESCO *World Heritage List 2012*

Leaders
- Central Intelligence Agency – Publications – World Leaders
- Business Inside, *The 15 Longest-Serving World Leaders* [Online]
- Parade, *World's Worst Dictators 2009* [Online]

Homicide
- UNODC, *Intentional homicide, count and rate per 100,000 population, 2010*
- UNODC, *UNODC study shows that homicide rates are highest in parts of the Americas and Africa* [Online]

Billionaires
- Forbes, *The World's Billionaires* [Online]
- Forbes, *Moscow Leads Cities With Most Billionaires* [Online]

Income
- OECD *Society at a Glance 2011*
- Forbes *2011 Rich List* [Online]
- United Nations World Vision

Clean Energy
- PEW Charitable Trusts, *Who's winning the clean energy race? 2010* [Online]

Leisure Time
- OECD Social Indicators, *Special Focus: Measuring Leisure in OECD Countries* [Online]

Life Expectancy
- Central Intelligence Agency World Factbook, 2011 – Country Comparison – Life Expectancy at Birth
- UN News Centre, *As world passes 7 billion milestone, UN urges action to meet key challenges* [Online]
- Daily Mail, *Dawn of a new age: The first person to reach 150 is already alive... and soon we'll live to be a THOUSAND, claims scientist*, 6 July 2011
- The Wall Street Journal, *Living to 100 and Beyond* [Online]

Access to Electricity
- The World Bank – Data – Climate Change – Access to Electricity (% of Population)
- IEA *Access to Electricity* [Online]

Arable Land
- Central Intelligence Agency World Factbook, 2011 – Land Use
- The Guardian, *Fears for the world's poor countries as the rich grab land to grow food*, 3 July 2009

Sex Life
- Durex Network, *The Face of Global Sex 2008: The path to sexual confidence* [Online]
- Durex Network, *The Face of Global Sex 2007 - First Sex: An opportunity of a lifetime* [Online]

Infant Mortality
- Central Intelligence Agency World Factbook, 2011 – Country Comparison – Infant Mortality Rate

Overseas Aid Recipients
- OECD, *Development Aid at a Glance – Statistics by Region 2012* [Online]
- The Guardian, *Aid from OECD countries - who gives the most and how has it changed?*, 6 April 2011

Nobel Prize Winners
- www.nobelprize.org

Economy
- Pew Global Attitudes Project, *China Seen Overtaking U.S. as Global Superpower* [Online]

Mammals
- The World Bank - Data – Environment – Mammal species, threatened
- The International Union for the Conservation of Nature (IUCN) *Red List* [Online]
- World Wildlife Fund [Online]

City Living
- World Health Organization - www.who.int/research/en/
- Popular Reference Bureau [Online]
- United Nations *2005 Population Growth and Challenges and Development Goals* [Online]

Nuclear Producers
- International Atomic Energy Agency, *Annual Report 2010* [Online]
- World Nuclear Association, *National Policies Radioactive Waste Management – Appendix 3* [Online]
- Seeking Alpha, *Where to Invest in the Upcoming Nuclear Renaissance* [Online]

Corruption
- The Guardian, *Corruption index 2010 from Transparency International: find out how each country compares*, 26 October 2010
- Transparency International, *Corruption Perceptions Index 2010* [Online]

Obesity
- WHO – Global Infobase
- WHO – Media Centre – Obese and Overweight

Religions
- Central Intelligence Agency World Factbook, 2011 – Religions

Newspaper
- Pew Global Attitudes Project [Online]

Old Age
- US Census Bureau, *An Aging World, 2008* [Online]
- United Nations, Population Division, *World Population Ageing 1950–2050* [Online]

Population
- Population Reference Bureau, *2011 World Population Data Sheet* [Online]
- United Nations, Population Division, *World Population to 2300* [Online]

Forests
- The World Bank – Data – Climate Change – Forest Area

Birth Rate
- Central Intelligence Agency World Factbook, 2011 – Country Comparison – Birth Rate
- United Nations, *White Paper: Probabilistic Projections of the Total Fertility Rate for All Countries for the 2010 World Population Prospects* [Online]

HIV
- United Nations Programme on HIV and AIDS *2008 Report on the global AIDS epidemic* [Online]
- UNAIDS *Report on the Global AIDS Epidemic 2010* [Online]

Mobile Phones
- Central Intelligence Agency World Factbook, 2011 – Telephones – Mobile Cellular
- Cisco *Visual Networking Index: Global Mobile Data Traffic Forecast Update, 2011–2016* [Online]
- Wireless Intelligence, *Global mobile connections surpass 5 billion milestone* [Online]

Arms Suppliers
- CRS Report for Congress, *Conventional Arms Transfers to Developing Nations, 2001–2008* [Online]
- The New York Times, *Despite Slump, US Role as Top Arms Supplier Grows*, 6 September 2009

Oil Reserves
- Central Intelligence Agency World Factbook, 2011 – Proved Reserves
- International Energy Agency 2009
- Forbes, *The Worst Oil Spills* [Online]

Water
- The World's Water, *Per-Capita Bottled Water Consumption by Top Countries, 1999–2010 (Liters per Person per Year)* [Online]
- Zenith International, *2007 Global bottled water maintains growth momentum* [Online]

Drug Use
- Public Library of Science, *Toward a Global View of Alcohol, Tobacco, Cannabis, and Cocaine Use: Findings from the WHO World Mental Health Surveys* [Online]
- UNODC, *World Drug Report 2011* [Online]
- *The World Mental Health Survey 2008*
- *Journal of Epidemiology and Community Health*, 'Intelligence across childhood in relation to illegal drug use in adulthood: 1970 British Cohort Study'

Olympics
- Olympic Games - www.olympic.org/olympic-games

Peace
- Global Peace Index 2011
- The Guardian, *Global peace index 2011: the full list*, 25 May 2011

Satisfaction
- World Values Survey, 2007, *Development, Freedom, and Rising Happiness – A Global Perspective (1981–2007)* [Online]
- Proceeding of the National Academy of Sciences, October 2011
- Social Science and Medicine

CO₂
- World Bank & Energy Information Adminstration, 2011
- The Guardian, *World carbon dioxide emissions data by country: China speeds ahead of the rest*, 31 January 2011

Online relationships
- Oxford Internet Institute, *A Global Shift in the Social Relationships of Networked Individuals: Meeting and Dating Online Comes of Age* [Online]

Women in Power
- Inter-Parliamentary Union, *Women in National Parliaments* [Online]

Refugees
- UNHCR Global Trends, 2010

Online News
- Pew Global Attitudes Project
- eBizMBA www.ebizmba.com/articles/news-websites
- BBC News, *Mail Online overtakes NY Times as top online newspaper* [Online]

Teenage Pregnancy
- WHO, *World Health Statistics 2010* [Online]
- WHO, *Young people: health risks and solutions* [Online]
- Unicef, *UNICEF: Extreme Risks for Pregnant Women and Newborn Babies in Developing Countries* [Online]

Happiness
- Leger Marketing, *On Marketing, 2011* [Online]

Road Fatalities
- IRTAD *Annual Report 2010*
- The Guardian, *The world's most dangerous roads - get the data*, 11 May 2011

Broadband
- OECD Communications Outlook – Table 8.4 Households with Broadband Access
- Point Topic, *World Broadband Statistics: Short Report Q3 2011* [Online]
- iSuppli, *Global Broadband Subscribers Set to Rise By Nearly 60 Percent by 2015* [Online]

Education
- Central Intelligence Agency World Factbook, 2011 – Education Expenditures
- United Nations *Millenium Development Goals*
- McKinsey and Co, 2010 [Online]

Firearms
- UNODC, *Percentage of homicides by firearm, number of homicides by firearm and homicides by firearm rate per 100,000 population* [Online]
- Small Arms Survey
- Inside World Football, *Brazil to exchange free World Cup tickets in return for illegal guns* [Online]

Marriage
- United Nations, Department of Economic and Social Affairs, Population Division – World Marriage Data 2008
- Nation Master, *Divorce rate (most recent) by country* [Online]
- The Telegraph, *Four kisses a day are key to long-lasting marriage, survey suggests*, 1 March 2009

Coco-Cola
- Coco-Cola Annual Review 2011

Fraud
- PricewaterhouseCoopers, *Cybercrime: protecting against the growing threat - Global Economic Crime Survey* [Online]

Languages
- Ethnologue – Statistical Summaries – Table 3: Languages with at least 3 million first-language speakers
- UN.org – UN At A Glance – UN Official Languages

Hours Online
- The Huffington Post, *The Top 11 Countries That Spend The Most Time Online* [Online]
- The World Bank – Data – Infrastructure – Internet Users (per 100 people)
- ITU, *ICT Facts and Figures 2011* [Online]
- ITU, *ITU releases latest global ICT pricing and penetration data* [Online]
- Jupiter Research, *US Entertainment and Media Consumer Survey, 2005* [Online]

Health
- OECD, *Public Health Spending: Public social expenditure as a percentage of GDP* [Online]
- World Health Organization, 2008
- WHO, *World Health Report 2000* [Online]
- Bloomberg Businessweek, *The Health of Nations* [Online]

Overseas Aid Donors
- OECD – Aid Statistics, Donor Aid Charts

Unemployment
- Central Intelligence Agency World Factbook, 2011 – Country Comparison – Unemployment Rate
- UN – Youth – Unemployment, 2009
- AFP, *Zimbabwe lifts foreign currency restrictions* [Online]
- ILO, *World of Work Report 2011 – ILO says world heading for a new and deeper jobs recession, warns of more social unrest* [Online]

Inflation
- The World Bank – Data – Economic Policy & External – Inflation, consumer prices (annual %) CNN, 2011
- China Daily, *Boosting yuan's flexibility* [Online]
- Library of Economics and Liberty, *Hyperinflation* [Online]

Suicide
- WHO – Suicide rates per 100,000 by country, year and sex (Table)
- WHO, *Suicide Prevention* [Online]

Smoking 15-years-olds
- OECD, *Society at a Glance 2009*
- WHO, *Health effects of smoking among young people* [Online]
- The Guardian, *Lebanon: the world capital for teen smokers*, 10 March 2009

Executions
- Amnesty International – Death Sentences and Executions 2010

Caesareans
- OECD - Health Care Utilization stats.oecd.org/Index. aspx?DataSetCode=HEALTH_PROC
- WHO, *Multiple strategies for decreasing caesarean section rates* [Online]
- The Lancet, *Maternal mortality for 181 countries, 1980–2008: a systematic analysis of progress towards Millennium Development Goal 5* [Online]

Violence Against Women
- OECD, *Family violence* [Online]
- WHO, *Violence against women by intimate partners* [Online]
- Family Violence Interventions for the Justice System
- Aurat Foundation, *Annual Report, 2010* [Online]

GDP per Capita
- The World Bank – Data – Economic Policy & External – GDP per capita (current US$)
- KPMG, *Funding NHI: A spoonful of sugar?* [Online]
- The Economist

Foreign Born Population
- OECD Factbook 2010: Economic, Environmental and Social Statistics
- United Nations *International Migration, 2006* [Online]

Prisons
- King's College London – International Centre for Prison Studies – World Prison Population List
- The New York Times, *U.S. prison population dwarfs that of other nations*, 23 April 2008

Alcohol
- WHO, *Alcohol* www.who.int/substance_abuse/facts/alcohol/en/index.html
- WHO, *Action needed to reduce health impact of harmful alcohol use*

% under 15
- Population Reference Bureau, *2011 World Population Data Sheet*
- The Independent, *Museveni watch out, the youth will change*
- Center for Social Development, *Innovations in Youth Saving and Asset Building around the World*

Fact pages sources

p. 22
- FAO Animal Production and Health Division *Challenges for a wealthier world: Meat for all?*
- The New York Times, *Rethinking the Meat-Guzzler*, 27 January 2008

p. 30
- The Economist, *In search of growth* [Online]
- The Economist, *The global debt clock* [Online]

p. 40
- UNODC – 2.2 Opium/heroin

p. 52
- NASA, *NASA Finds 2011 Ninth-Warmest Year on Record* [Online]

p. 64
- Population Reference Bureau, *World Population Data Sheet 2011* [Online]

p. 74
- The Age, *More iPhones sold per second than babies born* [Online]

p. 82
- GlobalSecurity.org, *The World at War* [Online]

p. 92
- Globalchange, *Human Appropriation of the World's Fresh Water Supply* [Online]

p. 100
- US Geological Survey – Earthquake Hazards Programme – Earthquake Facts and Statistics

p. 114
- Ecology Global Network – *World Birth and Death Rates* [Online]
- Population Reference Bureau, *World Population Data Sheet 2011* [Online]

p. 124
- Ecology Global Network – *World Birth and Death Rates* [Online]
- Population Reference Bureau, *World Population Data Sheet 2011* [Online]

p. 134
- *Bulletin of Atomic Scientists*, 2009

p. 148
- UN Habitat, *State of the World Cities 2010/2011* [Online]
- Press Conference by UN-Habitat on Conclusion of Fifth World Urban Congress

p. 162
- Earth System Research Laboratory – Trends in Atmospheric Carbon Dioxide;
- The Guardian, *Carbon levels hit new peak, research shows*, 31 May 2011

p. 174
- FAO, *Global Food Losses and Food Waste* [Online]